HARDPRESS.NET
HOME OF HARD-TO-FIND BOOKS

Hobart's Analysis of Bishop Butler's Analogy of Religion, Natural and Revealed, to the Consititution and Course of Nature. With Notes
by Richard Hobart

Address:
HardPress
8345 NW 66TH ST #2561
MIAMI FL 33166-2626
USA
Email: info@hardpress.net

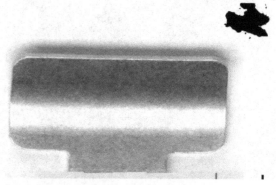

HOBART'S ANALYSIS OF

BISHOP BUTLER'S

ANALOGY OF RELIGION,

Natural and Revealed,

TO THE CONSTITUTION AND COURSE OF NATURE.

WITH NOTES.

ALSO, CRAUFURD'S QUESTIONS FOR EXAMINATION.

REVISED AND

HOBART'S ANALYSIS OF

BISHOP BUTLER'S

ANALOGY OF RELIGION,

Natural and Revealed,

TO THE CONSTITUTION AND COURSE OF NATURE.

WITH NOTES.

ALSO, CRAUFURD'S QUESTIONS FOR EXAMINATION.

REVISED AND

ADAPTED TO THE USE OF SCHOOLS.

BY CHARLES E. WEST,
PRINCIPAL OF RUTGERS INSTITUTE IN THE CITY OF NEW YORK.

NEW YORK:
HARPER & BROTHERS, PUBLISHERS,
82 CLIFF STREET.
1848.

ADVERTISEMENT.

An abridgment of Hobart's Analysis of Butler's Analogy, with questions for examination by Craufurd, was edited by me some three or four years since. From the favorable manner in which the work was received, I have been led to prepare another edition for the press, differing from the former in the following respects : 1st. The Analysis is given without abridgment. 2d. The Questions have not been introduced into the body of the text, but are appended at the end of the several chapters. This course has been adopted to meet the wishes of friends, some of whom have expressed the desire that there should be no interruption in the text by the introduction of questions ; while others have been pleased with the questions, and have preferred that they should be retained. By the arrangement adopted, it will be seen that the views of both have been met. The use of the questions is left at the option of the teacher. They can be dispensed with, if rigid attention is given to the synopsis, as presented at the beginning of each chapter. The combined study of both, however, will not be found unprofitable : the first, as giving a succinct outline of the argument ; the second, as leading to such explanations as are adapted to fix it in the mind of the learner. If the scholar will take the pains of studying the two in connection, he can not fail of mastering his task. This is the end which has been kept in view by the publication of this little work, and it is hoped that its introduction into Academies and Schools where Butler is studied will prove this effort at his elucidation not to have been unsuccessful.

CHARLES E. WEST.

Rutgers Institute, New York,
Feb. 26th, 1848.

PREFACE.

NOTWITHSTANDING the approbation with which this celebrated treatise of Bishop Butler has been received, his style has been frequently censured as intricate and obscure. A great portion of this obscurity should justly be attributed to the nature of the subject, and, perhaps, a greater degree of it to the comprehensive mind of the author, and the conciseness of expression characteristic of such minds. It can not be expected that difficulties of the former kind can be lessened by an analysis, or, indeed, by any thing else, without that serious attention in the reader which subjects of such importance demand—the removal of those of

A*

the latter class has here been attempted. For example, the scope and connection of the several parts not being sufficiently marked out; the length of elaborate sentences, where clauses are minutely opposed, or exceptions briefly adverted to; repetitions that separate, at great intervals, the parts of the reasoning; the introduction of digressionary remarks—all contribute to render it the more abstruse for ordinary perusal.

The summary at the head of each chapter, in this Analysis shows, at once, its design and the connection of the steps of reasoning employed in it. For the most part, the precise language of the original has been adhered to, so far as it did not come within the preceding exceptions. Some notes have been occasionally introduced from the text containing remarks unconnected with the chapter in which they stand, while others have been added of an explanatory nature.

It is distinctly to be kept in view, that the evidence of analogy is applied, not to the proof of religion natural or revealed, but to the confirmation of that proof supposed to be known.

"I know no author," says Dr. Reid, "who has made a more just and a more happy use of analogical reasoning than Bishop Butler, in his Analogy of Religion. In that excellent work, the author does not ground any of the truths of religion upon analogy as their proper evidence : he only makes use of analogy to answer objections against them. When objections are made against truths of religion, which may be made with equal strength against what we know to be true in the course of nature, such objections can have no weight." To the same purpose, it is observed by Dr. Campbell, that, "analogical evidence is generally more successful in silencing objections than in evincing truth. Though it rarely refutes, it frequently repels refutation ; like those weapons which, though they can not kill the enemy, will ward his blows."

It consequently follows, that if any point of the analogy appears weak, it is not to be concluded that the proper proofs of it are so. Some parts are more convincing than others ; but the force of this treatise can only be estimated by viewing all its parts in connection. The books of Nature and of Revelation are compared together.   An *Author of Nature* is the only point assumed ; and, by a reference to the natural course of things—to indisputable facts—to man himself, according to his original constitution—to his daily habit of acting on evidence far inferior to that which ac ompanies revelation—all objections are answered, as applying with equal force against the constitution of nature, where they are found false in fact. The objector is answered according to principles which he can not deny.   The part of his conduct which is natural convicts him of objecting to what is equally suited to his nature.

It is evident that the proper motives and principles of the Christian are not to be looked for in a work that descends so low ; for example, the nature of human life is such as to encourage any kind of exertion on the lowest chance of obtaining the end in view ; yet, although this may show the unreasonableness of neglect with regard to a future state, where the chance of its existence is acknowledged, this chance is not intended to be a substitute for that faith, which is " *the substance of things hoped for, and the evidence of things not seen.*"

Yet it is not to be inferred that the *believer* can not be confirmed by arguments from analogy. He also may have doubts which they can immediately dispel; and to all, even the most steadfast disciples of the Lord Jesus, they must afford some degree, if not of profit, at least of pleasure. It might be added, if the work were written on any other subject, that it would serve as a useful exercise to our intellectual faculties in and for itself; but, in this case, the end so far exceeds the means, that we must altogether lose sight of them in the all-important object to which they are directed.*

But the chief design of this treatise undoubtedly is, to warn the unbeliever and careless professor of the danger to which they are exposed, and to extort from their own breasts a confession of their self-condemnation; to show them

* I can not forbear adding a late encomium upon the works of the author of the Analogy :—"I am ready and anxious to acknowledge," observes Dr. O'Brien, "that I trace so distinctly to his (Bishop Butler's) writings the origin of the soundest and clearest views that I possess upon the nature of the human mind, that I could not write on this or any kindred subject, without a consciousness that I was, directly or indirectly, borrowing largely from him."—*Vide Two Sermons on the Human Nature of Christ.*

that there is more even in *natural* religion, and
much more in *revealed* religion, than they suppose ; and to lead them to search the Scriptures of truth.   It is humbly hoped that the
present Analysis may prove useful with respect to such persons where the abstruseness
of the original work might render it less ef-
ficient, or even, in some degree, prevent its
perusal.

CONTENTS.

CONTENTS.

PART II.

OF REVEALED RELIGION.

INTRODUCTION.

I. PROBABLE evidence is essentially distinguished from demonstrative by this—that it admits of degrees—from the *highest moral certainty* to the *very lowest presumption.* But the *very lowest presumption* does not prove a thing to be *probably true;* especially if (as there may be probabilities on both sides) there are any probabilities against it; yet it partakes of the nature of probability, for by frequent repetition, it will amount to *moral certainty.* Thus, the observation of the ebb and flow of the tide to-day begets a very low presumption that it *may* happen to-morrow; but this observation often repeated gives us a full assurance that it will.

B

II. From observing a likeness in this event to another which has come to pass, we determine on the probability of its occurrence, and so of every thing else.* Therefore, the foundation of probability is expressed in the word "likely" (*verisimile*), like some truth, or true event, in itself, or in its evidence, or in some of its circumstances; and thus it daily happens that we have a *presumption*, an *opinion*, or *full conviction* of the truth of an event, past or future, according to the frequency of the observation of a similar one under similar circumstances. For example, we conclude that a child, if it lives twenty years, will grow up to the stature and strength of a man—that food will contribute to the preservation of its life, and the want of it, for such a number of days, will be its certain destruction. Whether we judge, expect, hope, or fear, we are guided by the same principle of observed similarity.

III. But the extent of our observation being

* Though the common experience of the ordinary course of things have justly a mighty influence on the minds of men, to make them give or refuse credit to any thing proposed to their belief, yet there is *one case* wherein the strangeness of the fact lessens not the assent to a fair testimony given of it. For where such supernatural events are suitable to ends aimed at by Him who has the power to change the course of nature, there, under such circumstances, they *may be fitter to procure belief*, by *how much the more they are beyond or contrary to ordinary observation*. This is the proper case with miracles, which, well attested, do not only find credit themselves, but give it also to other truths which need such confirmation.—*Locke.*

limited, it may warrant a fair conclusion in the way of analogy, though a *false one*. Thus the prince who lived in a warm climate,* who had never seen water but in a fluid state, naturally inferred that there was no such thing as water becoming hard.† The field of our observation being more extended, we do not consider this any presumption against the possibility of water being frozen. We know that it is *supposable* that there may be frost in England any given day in January next, and *probable* on some day in that month, and *morally certain* some time or other in the winter. Therefore, probable evidence, in its very nature, affords but an imperfect kind of information.

IV. It relates only to beings of limited capacities.

* A Dutch embassador, entertaining the King of Siam with the particularities of Holland, which he was inquisitive after, among other things, told him that the water in his country would sometimes, in cold weather, be so hard that men walked upon it, and that it would bear an elephant if it were there. To which the king replied, "Hitherto I have believed the strange things you have told me, because I look upon you as a sober, fair man, but now I am sure you lie."— *Locke*.

† But it has been well observed, by Dr. Leland, that *experience may assure us that facts or events are possible, but not that the contrary is impossible*. The greatest uniformity and frequency of experience can not prove the *certainty* of an event, nor even afford the least *probability* that it would *never* happen otherwise. For aught we know, there may be occasions on which it would fail, and secret causes in the frame of things which sometimes may counteract these by which it is produced.

Every thing is *certain* to an Infinite Intelligence, for every thing must be observed by Him absolutely as it is in itself, certainly true or certainly false; but with us most things are only probable. In questions of real or imaginary difficulty, the lowest presumption on one side more than on the other determines the question; and, in the common pursuits of life, even in questions of great consequence, we find men considering themselves bound to act not only where there are merely slight probabilities *in favor* of success, but when these are *equalled*, or even *exceeded*, by probabilities *against* their succeeding.

V. But whence is it that *likeness* produces a presumption, opinion, or full conviction? And how can we be certain that the conclusion drawn by analogy is correct? This belongs to the subject of logic, and is a part of that subject which has not yet been thoroughly considered; but it is evident (and enough for the present purpose) that this general way of arguing is natural, just, and conclusive; for there is no man can make a question but that the sun will rise to-morrow,* and be

---

* "A man brought into being at maturity and placed in a desert island would abandon himself to despair when he first saw the sun set and the night come on: for he could have no expectation that ever the day would be renewed. But he is transported with joy when he again beholds the glorious orb appearing in the east, and the heavens and the earth illuminated as before. He again views the declining sun with ap-

seen, where it is seen at all, in the figure of a circle, and not in that of a square.

VI. For introducing this sort of reasoning into the subject of *revealed* religion, we have the authority of Origen, who has observed, that " he who believes the Scripture to have proceeded from Him who is the Author of nature, may well expect to find the same sort of difficulties in it as are found in the constitution of nature." And it may be added, that he who denies the Divine origin of the one, on account of these difficulties, may, with as much reason, deny that of the other. We argue from the likeness that exists between the revealed and the natural dispensation of Providence, that they have both the same Author; at least, that the objections against it are of no force, from difficulties in the one analogical or similar to what are found in the other, which is *acknowledged* to be from God, *for an Author of nature is here* SUPPOSED (and to this assumption there can be no objection,

prehension, yet not without hope : the second night is less dismal than the first, but is still very uncomfortable on account of the weakness of the probability produced by one favorable instance. As the instances grow more numerous, the probability becomes stronger and stronger: yet it may be questioned, whether a man in these circumstances would ever arrive at so high a degree of moral certainty in this matter as we experience, who know not only that the sun has risen every day since we began to exist, but also that the same phenomenon has happened regularly for more than five thousand years, without failing in a single instance.—*Beattie on Truth.*

B*

since it is not denied by the generality of those who profess themselves dissatisfied with the evidences of religion ; and if it were, as there is no presumption against it prior to the proof of it, so it has been often proved, with accumulated evidence, from final causes, abstract reasonings, tradition, the general consent of mankind, &c., &c.).

VII. As to the degree of weight to be attached to this argument from analogy, in some cases it will amount to a practical proof—in others merely a confirmation of what can be otherwise proved ; yet its chief force will be to answer the objections against the *system* both of natural and revealed religion, and it will possess considerable force in answering objections against the *evidence* of it—the argument being conclusive in proportion to the degree of the whole analogy or likeness. It is to be distinctly observed that, in this analogy, we argue from known existing *facts* to others that are like them.

VIII. This has been shown to be a method of proof, practical, usual, and conclusive in various degrees. It does not argue from *hypothesis*, or from the *possibility* to the *propriety* of a better form of Divine government. Those who argue from hypothesis, reason either from *assumed* principles, or from *certain* principles *assumed to be applicable* to cases to which they have no ground to apply them. The former resemble Des Cartes building a world upon hypothesis; the others act like those who explain the structure of the human body from mere mathematics, without sufficient data. As to those who run into the wild extravagance of planning an improved state of things, the plan fixed on by the wisest speculator probably would not be the very best, even according to his own notion of "best." For what would he propose? That which, both by occasions and motives, was productive of the greatest virtue, or greatest happiness, or both combined; *i. e.*, when fully expressed, that all creatures should, at first, be made as perfect and as happy as they were capable of being; that nothing—at least nothing of hazard or danger—should be put upon them to do; or that they should, in fact, always do what was right and most conducive to happiness. And how would he effect this? He would do away with the method of government by punishment, as absurd and contrary to happiness; and he would either not give them any principles which would endanger their doing wrong, or he would lay the right motive of action before them in so strong a manner as would never fail of inducing them to act conformably to it. We may at once give this General Answer: Following the first principles of our nature, we unavoidably judge some ends to be preferable to others; and our whole nature leads us to ascribe all moral perfection to

God, and to deny all imperfection of Him ; this is a practical proof of His moral character, for it is the voice of God speaking in us ; from hence we conclude that virtue and happiness are essentially united, and that under His government right must prevail. But the necessary *means* of accomplishing this end, we have not faculties to determine. Even in the little affairs of this present life, we are not competent judges, and we are likely to be much less so in a system of such extent as this world may be, taking in all that is past and to come, though we should suppose it detached from the whole creation.

We shall first apply the argument from analogy to the foundation of all our hopes and fears—a future life.

QUESTIONS—INTRODUCTION.

1. How is *probable* evidence distinguished from *demonstrative*; and to what may the former at length amount? Illustrate this by a fact in nature.

2. What exception does Locke justly produce to the following general rule, namely: that from observing a likeness in an event to another which has come to pass, we determine on the probability of its occurrence and so of every thing else?

3. What imperfection naturally attaches itself to our reasoning by analogy, from the extent of our observation being limited? Quote Dr. Leland's observation as to the exact value of experience, in reasoning upon a reported fact.

4. How do men act in all worldly affairs, with respect to probable evidence?

5. Quote the argument from Beattie by which he endeavors to prove that *likeness* would produce presumption, then opinion, lastly conviction.

6. What does Origen say upon the application of analogy to religion? How does Butler support and confirm his argument?

7. What degree of weight is to be attached to the argument from analogy; and in what consists its principal excellence?

8. What general answer may we give to those who would argue from the *possibility* to the *propriety* of a better than the existing form of Divine government?

SCHEME OF PART I.

ON NATURAL RELIGION.

CHAP. I. Analogy fully confirms the Scripture account of the existence of a Future State—

CHAP. II. And that it will be one of Rewards and Punishments—

CHAP. III. And that these Rewards and Punishments will be dispensed according to the merit and demerit of our actions.

CHAP. IV. Therefore it becomes incumbent on us to resist all Temptations in this *State of Trial.*

CHAP. V. And to make use of all the Means of Improvement for another Life, which this Probation State affords as intended for *Moral Discipline.*

CHAP. VI. For these Obligations are not in the least degree affected by the opinion of Universal Necessity.

CHAP. VII. Or by any objections which may be urged against God's Moral Government.

PART I.

OF NATURAL RELIGION.

CHAPTER I.

ON A FUTURE STATE.

I. A Future State probable from the Changes which we have undergone.

II. And from the probability of our continuing endued with the same Capacities, unless there be some ground for supposing that Death will destroy us—we have no ground from Analogy or Reason, and we can not have it from any thing else.

III. Yet there are *Imaginary* Presumptions founded on the notion of Living Beings being Compounded, and therefore divisible. A proof of the Contrary confirmed by a general Observation from Experience, leading to four particular Observations. An Objection to some of these, "that they tend to prove the immortality of Brutes," answered.

IV. A contrary Analogy proved to be only apparent.

V. Our entrance on another State shown to be natural.

C

I. Passing by the difficulties raised by some concerning personal identity,* the probability of a future state appears from the changes we have undergone—from the imperfect state of infancy to mature
age. Nor is this a law of *our* being only, that we
should exist at one period of our life with capacities of action, of enjoyment, and suffering greatly
different from those at another period of it; we
find it in other creatures also; for example, the
change of worms into flies—birds and insects burst-
ing the shell, and, by this means, entering into a
new world. But, as far as we are concerned, that
there should be a future state of existence, as dif-

---

* To the Analogy are usually subjoined two dissertations,
both originally inserted in the body of the work. One on
Personal Identity, in which are contained some strictures
on Mr. Locke, who asserts that consciousness makes or constitutes *Personal Identity*; whereas, as our author observes,
consciousness makes only *Personality*, or is necessary to the
idea of a person, *i. e.*, a thinking, intelligent being; but presupposes, and therefore can not constitute, personal identity;
just as knowledge, in any other case, presupposes truth, but
does not constitute it. Consciousness of *past* actions does
indeed show us the identity of ourselves, or gives us a certain assurance that we are the same persons or living agents
now which we were at the time to which our remembrance
can look back : but still we should be the same persons as
we were, though this consciousness of what is past were
wanting, though all that had been done by us formerly were
forgotten—unless it be true that no person has existed a
single moment beyond what he can remember. The other
dissertation is on the Nature of Virtue, which does not belong to the religious, but to the moral, system of our author.
—*Bishop Halifax.*

ferent from the present as the present is from our state in the womb and in infancy, is only what is warranted by the analogy of nature.

II. Secondly, from the probability of our continuing endued with the same capacities of action, happiness, and misery which we feel that we now possess. This is probable, unless there be some ground for supposing that death will destroy them; for, in any thing, existence leads to a probability of *continuance*, except where we have some reason to think it will be altered. This seems to be our only reason for believing that any one substance now existing will continue to exist a moment longer (the self-existent substance only excepted). There is the same *kind* of probability, though not the same *degree* of it, that our living powers will continue after death as there is that our substances will; and there would be no probability against the former, if men were assured that the unknown event, death, was not the destruction of our faculties of perception and action; *i. e.*, there would be no probability against it arising from any thing else, unconnected with death, being able to destroy them. Now, if *death* be justly presumed to destroy them, and if this be not merely a confused suspicion, we must have some ground for the presumption from the reason of the thing, or from the analogy of nature. First, we have it not from the reason of the thing, for we know not what death is in it-

self, but only some of its effects, such as the dissolution of flesh, skin, and bones; we know not upon
what the exercise (much less the existence) of our
living powers depends; for they may exist without
being exercised, and when there is no present capacity of exercising them, as in a sleep or swoon.
They may depend on something out of the reach
of the King of Terrors; so that there is nothing
more certain than that the reason of the thing
shows us no connection between death and the
destruction of living agents.*   Secondly, we have
it not from the analogy of nature, for, throughout
the whole of it, there is not the slightest presumption that animals *ever* lose their living powers—
much less, if possible, by *death*.   This event destroys the sensible proof which we had before their
death, of their being possessed of living powers,
but does not appear to afford the least reason to

---

* *Destruction of living powers*, is a manner of expression
unavoidably ambiguous, and may signify either *the destruction of a living being, so as that the same living being shall
be incapable of ever perceiving or acting again at all*, or *the
destruction of those means and instruments by which it is capable of its* present *life, of its* present *state of perception, and
of action*.   It is here used in the former sense.   When it is
used in the latter, the epithet *present* is added.   The loss of
a man's eye is a destruction of living powers in the *latter*
sense; but we have no reason to think the destruction of
living powers, in the *former* sense, to be possible.   We have
no more reason to think a being endued with living powers,
ever loses them during his whole existence than to believe
that a stone ever acquires them.—*Butler.*

believe that they are then, or by that event, deprived of them.   As far as our faculties can trace, they retain them, and this is in itself a probability of their retaining them beyond that period, especially when viewed in connection with our first proof.

III. *Objected against the assertion that " there is no proof from the reason of the thing."*   " Living beings are compounded, and so divisible."

ANSWER. There is no proof of this; it arises not from reason, but from that delusive faculty—useful, indeed, to apprehension, but the author of all error —Imagination.   Since consciousness is indivisible, it should rather seem that the perceptive power, and consequently the subject in which it resides, must be so too.†   As a particle of matter (as well as its power of motion) is one and indivisible, if its motion be absolutely one and indivisible—for if the

---

* There is no subject on which doubts and difficulties may not be started by ingenious and disputatious man; and therefore from the number of their objections, and the length of the controversy to which they give occasion, we can not, in any case, conclude that the original evidence is weak, or even that it is not obvious and striking.   Were we to presume that every principle is dubious against which specious objections may be contrived, we should be quickly led into universal skepticism.   The two ways in which the ingenuity of speculative men has been most commonly employed are dogmatical assertions of doubtful opinions, and *subtle cavils against certain truths.—Gerard's Dissertation*, II., 4.

† See Dr. Clarke's Letter to Dodwell, and the defenses of it.

particle were divisible, one part might be moved
and the other at rest, and thus its motion could not
be as is supposed—in the same way, if the subject
of consciousness be divisible, the consciousness of
our own existence would be divisible; so that one
part would be here and another there, contrary to
what is supposed and experienced.* Hence the
absolute oneness of the living agent renders the
body unessential to its being, and our organized
bodies are no more ourselves, or part of ourselves,
than any other matter around us; and yet it is as
easy to conceive how such matter may be appro-
priated to our use in the manner that our present
bodies are, as how we receive impressions from,
and have power over *any* matter. It is as easy to
conceive that we may exist out of bodies as in
them; that we might have animated bodies, of any
other organs and senses, wholly different from those
now given us, and that we may hereafter animate

* That it is highly unreasonable and absurd to suppose
the soul made up of innumerable consciousnesses, as matter
is necessarily made up of innumerable parts; and, on the
contrary, that it is highly reasonable to believe the *seat of
thought* to be a simple substance such as can not naturally be
divided and crumbled into pieces, as all matter is manifestly
subject to be, must, of necessity, be confessed. Consequently
the soul will not be liable to be dissolved at the dissolution
of the body, and, therefore, it will naturally be immortal. All
this seems to follow, at least, with the highest degree of
probability, from the single consideration of the soul's being
endued with sense, thought, or consciousness.—*Clarke's Evidence of Natural and Revealed Religion.*

these same or new bodies, variously modified and
organized, as to conceive how we can animate such
bodies as our present.   Their destruction, then,
might be like that of any other matter, without any
tendency to destroy our living powers.   Even without determining whether our living substances be
material or immaterial, all this is confirmed (though
from the nature of the case not properly proved)
by observations from experience.   We remain the
same living agents after the loss of our limbs, organs of sense, or even the greatest part of our
bodies ; we can remember ourselves the same when
our bodies were extremely small, and we lose now,
and might have lost then, a great part of our bodies,
and yet remain the same.   And it is certain, that
the bodies of all animals are in a constant change
from that never-ceasing attrition which there is in
every part of them.   All this leads us to distinguish
the large quantity of matter in which we are nearly interested from the living agent who remains one
and the same permanent being.

OBJECTION. What is alienated or lost is no part
of our original solid body, but only adventitious
matter.

ANSWER. Surely entire limbs which we may lose
must contain many solid parts and vessels of the
original body ; or, if this be not admitted, we have
no proof that any of these solid parts are dissolved
or alienated by death.

From this it follows :——1st. Even though the living being be not absolutely indivisible, yet it can not be assumed that death will be the dissolution of it until its proper bulk be determined, and till it be determined to be larger than the solid elementary particles of matter, which there is no ground to think any natural power can dissolve. 2dly. Our *interest* in systems of matter does not imply the destruction of ourselves the living agents, for we have, though not to the same *degree*, the *like* interest in all foreign matter, which gives us ideas, and over which we have any power ; nor have we any ground to conclude that any other systems of matter, suppose *internal* systems, are the living agents themselves ; for we can have no reason to conclude this, except from the same principle——our *interest* in such systems. 3d. If we consider the component parts of our body, this will more clearly appear. Our *organs of sense* and *our limbs* are only instruments which the living persons ourselves make use of to perceive and move with ; and therefore we have no other *kind* of relation to them than we have to any other foreign matter formed into instruments of perception and motion——suppose into a microscope and a staff. But are not our *organs* themselves percipient ? No ; the common optical experiments show that we see with our eyes in the same sense that we see with glasses ; and the like may justly be concluded from analogy of all our other senses.

Some of these organs may be lost, while the living beings, the former occupiers, remain unimpaired. In dreams we have a *latent* power, and, what would otherwise be an *unknown* power, of perceiving sensible objects in as strong and lively a manner without our external organs of sense as with them. But are not our *limbs* endued with the power of moving and directing themselves? No; a man can move an artificial leg, for example, as he used to move his natural one, only that the natural instrument of motion was more exactly formed, so as to move and produce motion in its several parts; his active power remains unlessened. And thus the finding that the dissolution of matter in which living beings were most nearly interested is not their dissolution, and that the destruction of several of the organs and instruments of perception and of motion is not their destruction, shows, demonstratively, that there is no ground to think that the dissolution of any other matter, or destruction of any other organs and instruments, will be the dissolution or destruction of living agents, from the *like* kind of relation. And we have no reason to think we stand in any *other* kind of relation to any thing which we find dissolved by death.

OBJECTION. Brutes, in the same way, might be proved to be immortal, and, by consequence, capable of everlasting happiness.

ANSWER. (1st.) In a *moral* point of view, no such

consequence necessarily follows as that they should
be capable of everlasting happiness; and, even admitting it, there is no difficulty; for we know not
what latent capacities they may be endued with;
and it is a general law of nature, that beings should
possess capacities of virtue for some time without
exercising them, as in infancy and childhood, and
often without exercising them at all in this world.
(2dly.) As to a *natural* immortality, the economy
of the universe may require living creatures without any capacities of this kind. Therefore we
must know the whole system before such can be
an objection to this part of the proof of the immortality of the human soul: it is less applicable
to the next part, which is more peculiar to man.
(3dly.) Our present powers of reflection not being dependent on our gross bodies in the manner
in which our organs of sense are, we may conclude
that they are not destroyed by death. We can
live in a state of reflection, after ideas are gained,
when none of our senses are affected or appetites
gratified, and in this state enjoy the greatest pleasure, or feel the greatest pain, without any assistance from our senses, and without any at all, which
we know of, from that body which will be destroyed by death. Further, there are some mortal diseases which do not affect, and, therefore, it may
be presumed, will not destroy our present intellectual powers. Indeed, the *body* and *intellectual*

powers mutually affecting each other would no more
prove the necessity of their joint dissolution than
the connection of the *body* and the *living agent* required *their* joint destruction, as already shown;
but instances of their *not* affecting each other afford
a presumption of the contrary. Several things, indeed, greatly affect all our living powers, and at
length suspend the exercise of them—as, for instance, drowsiness increasing till it ends in sound
sleep; and from hence we might have imagined it
would destroy them, till we found, by experience,
the weakness of this way of judging. But by these
diseases there is not even a shadow of probability
that our present reflecting powers will be destroyed. And if death, by diseases of this kind, is not
their destruction, it will scarcely be thought that
death by any other means is; and as it does not
destroy, it is probable it does not interrupt the *continuance* of the exercise of these powers, since they
can be exercised without the aid of the body, and in
a most lively manner, during the whole progress of
a mortal disease; nay, it may even remove the *hin-
derance* to our existing in a higher state of reflection,* namely, those external organs which render us
capable of existing in our present state of sensation, so that it may in some respects answer to our

---

* There are three distinct questions relating to a future
life here considered : Whether death be the destruction of
living agents ? if not, whether it be the destruction of their

birth,* not a suspension, but a continuation of our former faculties, with *great alterations.*

IV. *Objected against the assertion that " there is no proof from analogy."*   There is an analogy for death being the destruction of living creatures— namely, the decay of vegetables.

Answer. This comparison may be just enough for poetic similes, but not for an analogy ; for one of the two subjects compared is wholly void of that which is the chief thing in the other, and which is the only thing about the continuance of which we are inquiring—the power of perception and of action.†

V. Thus, when we go out of this world, we may pass into new scenes, and a new state of life and action, just as *naturally* as we came into the present ; for it would be a contradiction to say, that

present powers of reflection, as it certainly is the destruction of their present powers of sensation ? and if not, whether it be the suspension or discontinuance of the exercise of these present reflecting powers?   Now, if there be no reason to believe the last, there will be, if that were possible, less for the next, and less still for the first.—*Butler.*

* This, according to Strabo, was the opinion of the *Brachmans.*

† St. Paul answers objections against the resurrection, by analogy from the works of nature.   *Vide* 1 Cor., xv., 36. "The seed dies—it is only the germ or bud that springs ; the body of the seed first feeds this bud, and then turns to corruption."   It is particularly to be noted, that St. Paul is not speaking of the *identity* of the raised bodies.—*Vide Whitby on the passage.*

no state is *natural* but the *present*, and yet that the probability of a *future* one appears from reason. The meaning of the word *natural* is, *stated, fixed*, or *settled;* since what is natural as much requires and presupposes an Intelligent Agent to render it so, *i. e.*, to effect it *continually*, or at stated times, as what is supernatural or miraculous does to effect it *for once.* And from hence it must follow, that our notion of what is natural will be enlarged in proportion to our greater knowledge of the works of God, and the dispensations of His Providence. And this state may naturally be a social one, and the advantages of it—advantages of every kind may naturally be bestowed, according to some fixed general laws of wisdom, upon every one in proportion to the degrees of his virtue.

NOTE. The credibility of a future life, which has been here insisted upon, seems to answer all the purposes of religion. Even a *demonstrative* proof of *it* would not be a proof of *religion;* for it is just as reconcilable with the scheme of Atheism as the fact that we are now alive; but as religion implies a future state, presumptions against the latter would be urged against the former, and, therefore, it was necessary to remove them.

D

QUESTIONS—CHAPTER I.

1. Describe at full length the *scheme* of the first part of the Analogy which treats on *natural* religion.

2. How does Butler correct Locke in his definition of *personal identity?*

3. How does the analogy of Nature warrant us to assert that a future and different state of existence is probable?

4. Why is it probable that we may continue endued with the same capacities, unless they may be destroyed by death?

5. Show that there is no ground, from reason or from analogy, to presume that death does *destroy* any faculty of perception or action.

6. What answer can be given in refutation of the objection that "Living beings are compounded, and so divisible," and consequently liable to complete-destruction?

7. By what argument do we arrive at the following conclusion: viz., "That the dissolution of matter in which living beings were most *nearly interested*, is not *their* dissolution?" And to the proof of what truth is this conclusion applied?

8. Show that there is no probability that death will cause the destruction of our *present* powers of reflection.

9. Explain what is meant by the assertion that, "Our entrance on another state will be natural."

10. Show that the credibility of a future life, insisted on by Butler in this chapter, answers all the purposes of religion that a *demonstrative* proof would.

CHAPTER II.

ON THE GOVERNMENT OF GOD BY REWARDS AND PUN-ISHMENTS, AND PARTICULARLY ON THE LATTER.

I. If a Future State were only as credible as the last Chapter proves it to be, yet it is sufficient to urge us seriously to inquire, whether it is to be a State of Rewards and Punishments, depending upon our Conduct here? The probability of this appears from our happiness, and, in a great measure, our misery, in this life, being left dependent on our own actions; and objections to it are answered.

II. That there is to be a Future State of *Punishments,* appears from several particular analogies.

I. THE importance of the *question* concerning a future life arises from our capacity of happiness and misery. But the *consideration* of this question would appear of so little importance as only to be brought into our thoughts by curiosity concerning the mortality of others, or the near prospect of our own, if there were not a supposition of our happiness and misery hereafter depending upon our actions here.

That there is a future state of rewards and punishments, appears from the following General Analogy—We are at present under such a government; all that we enjoy, and a *great part* of what we suffer, *is put in our own power ;* for pleasure and pain are the consequences of our actions, and we are endued, by the Author of our nature, with capacities of foreseeing the consequences.   Our *preservation,* and every kind and degree of our *enjoyment,* is effected *by the means* of our own actions. Generally (though not always) our *sufferings* are produced by our own actions, though instruction, example, and experience forewarned us that the effect of such conduct would be injurious to our reputation, our property, or our life.   But why is the happiness and misery of creatures left dependent on themselves ?   Perhaps any other course would, from the nature of things, be impossible, or would confer a less degree of happiness, or not answer the end of an infinitely Perfect Mind, which may be pleased with the moral piety of moral agents in and for itself, as well as on account of its being a means of conferring happiness, or, perhaps, it would not answer the *whole* end of the Deity, which our faculties can not discern.   But is not the dispensation of happiness and misery in this world to be ascribed to the general course of nature ? True, this is the very point asserted; it is to be ascribed to the *general course,* and, therefore, to the *Author* of nature ; for we must not deny that He does things at all, because He does them constantly—because the effects of His acting are permanent,

whether His acting be so or not, though there is no
reason to think it is not.   The natural course of
things is the appointment of God; our natural
faculties, which guide us in our actions, by ena-
bling us to foresee their effects, are given by Him
also; the consequences of our actions are, therefore, His appointment, and the foresight of these
consequences a warning given us by Him how we
are to act; so that we are at present actually under His government in the strictest sense—in such
a sense as that He rewards and punishes us for our
actions—in the same sense as that we are under
the government of civil magistrates.   Because the
annexing pleasure to some actions and pain to
others in our power to do or forbear, and giving
notice of this appointment beforehand to those
whom it concerns, is the proper formal notion of
government.   It matters not, in this case, whether
the Deity interpose or not.   If civil magistrates
could make offenders execute their laws upon
themselves, or could execute them some other way,
without interposing at all, we should be under
their government in the same sense then as we are
now, but in a much higher degree and more perfect manner.   1st. Objected: Is the pleasure, then,
naturally accompanying every *particular* gratification of passion, intended as an inducement and a
reward for the gratification of it in every such particular instance ?   No, certainly; no more than our

eyes, which were unquestionably given us to see with, were intended to give us the sight of each particular object to which they do or can extend, however destructive of them, or however improper. 2d. Objected : Is every trifling pain an instance of Divine punishment ?   The *general* thing here asserted can not be evaded, without denying all final causes ; for if pleasure and pain be annexed to actions, as apparent inducements for our conduct, they must be admitted as instances of final causes. and as rewards and punishments.   If, for example, the pain felt on approaching too near the fire be intended to prevent our doing what tends to our destruction, this is as much an instance of God's punishing our actions, as if He did after having warned us by a voice from heaven.

II. A future state of *punishment*, being what men chiefly object against (either from *man's* nature being so frail and exposed to temptation as almost to annihilate the guilt of human vice, or from the nature of *God*, irresistible in His will, or incapable of offense and provocation), will appear farther credible from the following particular analogies between the punishments in this life and what religion teaches us of those in the next :—

" 1st. Natural punishments often follow actions that are accompanied with present gratification ; for example, sensual pleasure followed by sickness and untimely death.

2d. The punishments are often much greater than the present pleasures or advantages.

3d. The punishments are often delayed a great while, sometimes till long after the actions occasioning them are forgotten, contrary to what we might imagine, that they would *immediately* follow crimes or *not at all*.

4th. After such delay, these punishments often come, not by degrees, but suddenly, with violence and at once.

5th. Though these punishments, in very many cases, inevitably follow at the appointed time, yet persons have seldom a distinct full expectation, and, in many cases, see, or *may* see, only the credibility of their following : *e. g.*, that intemperance will bring after it diseases.

6th. The thoughtlessness and imprudence of youth does not prevent the punishments of excess following, and continuing the whole course of their existence in this life. These consequences are generally not considered, and can seldom be properly said to be believed beforehand.

7th. There are frequent punishments for want of acquirements, which being neglected at the natural season of acquiring, could not be acquired afterward : this is very observable in the natural course of things. The indocility of youth makes the consequent defects of old age irretrievable; the neglect of the seed time brings with it the irrecoverable loss of the whole year. There is a time when real reformation may prevent the consequences of extravagance; ascend to a higher degree, and there is no place for repentance.

8th. The punishments of neglect from inconsiderateness are often as dreadful as those of any active misbehavior from the most extravagant passion.

9th. Civil government being natural, its punishments are so too, and some of these capital; as the effects of a dissolute course of pleasure are often mortal. So that many *natural* punishments are final,* and seem inflicted naturally to diminish the aggregate of mischief, either by the removal of the offender from such a course, or by his example.

These things are so analogous to what religion teaches us concerning the future punishment of the wicked, that both would naturally be expressed in the same words. So much so, that it is doubtful to which of the two, principally, the following passage from the book of Proverbs, i., 22–32 refers: —Wisdom is introduced as frequenting the most public places of resort, and as rejected when she

---

* It can not be said that it is Scripture only, and not natural religion, which informs us of a future state of punishment, and the duration and degree of it. For this was known to the heathen poets and moralists; and reason might well conclude that it would be finally, and upon the whole, ill with the wicked. But what is peculiar to revelation is, it fixes the time when this distributive justice shall take place; namely, at the end of this world.—*Butler.*

offers herself as the natural appointed guide of human life—"How long, ye simple ones, will ye love simplicity? and the scorners delight in their scorning, and fools hate knowledge? Turn ye at my reproof; behold, I will pour out my Spirit unto you, I will make known my words unto you. Because I have called, and ye refused; I have stretched out my hand, and no man regarded; but ye have set at nought all my counsel, and would none of my reproof: I also will laugh at your calamity; I will mock when your fear cometh; when your fear cometh as desolation, and your destruction cometh as a whirlwind; when distress and anguish cometh upon you: then shall they call upon me, but I will not answer; they shall seek me early, but they shall not find me: for that they hated knowledge, and did not choose the fear of the Lord: they would none of my counsel: they despised all my reproof: therefore shall they eat of the fruit of their own way, and be filled with their own devices. For the turning away of the simple shall slay them, and the prosperity of fools shall destroy them."

The *instances* of punishments now mentioned* (for men are not always punished here in proportion to their sins) are sufficient to show what the

---

* Hence may be deduced experimental answers to many popular objections and excuses; as, that God is too *merciful* to inflict everlasting punishment; that we were *sincere* in our intentions; that we did not *know* it was a sin we were committing, &c. Our misery, like our neglect, is self-induced.

laws of the universe may admit, and to answer the
usual objections against a future state of punishment.   Indeed, nothing but a universally acknowledged *demonstration* on the side of Atheism can
justify unconcern about such a state.   The folly
of such security without proof appears from the
following analogy.   May it not be said of any person upon his being born into the world, that he
may act in such a manner as to be of no service to
it but by being made an example of the woful effects of vice and folly; he may bring death upon
himself from the hands of civil justice, or from the
effects of his excesses; or infamy and diseases worse
than death.   So that even with regard to the present
world, it had been better for him that he had never
been born.   And shall we suppose that there is no
danger of something similar in a future state, under
the providence and government of the same God,
though we rest as secure and act as licentiously as
we please ?

QUESTIONS—CHAPTER II.

1. What supposition makes the consideration of the question, concerning a future life, *evidently important* to each individual ?

2. Describe the *general analogy,* which makes a future state of rewards and punishments perfectly probable.

3. Why is the *present* happiness or misery of crea tures left so much dependent upon themselves ?

4. Suppose it to be granted that " The dispensation of happiness and misery, in this world, is to be ascribed to the *general course of nature,"* what follows from that admission ?

5. What is the *proper formal* notion of *government,* whether human or divine ?   And what would be the most *perfect manner* of it ?

6. State the two objections urged against the assertion that " pleasure or pain is annexed by God to certain actions as an apparent inducement for our conduct," and refute them.

7. Describe at full length the particular instances of analogy between natural punishments *in this life,* and what religion teaches us of those *in the next.*

8. For what purposes are the above-mentioned instances of analogy amply sufficient ?

9. By what analogy may the folly of a person, who is unconcerned about a future state, be demonstrated ?

CHAPTER III.

OF THE MORAL GOVERNMENT OF GOD.

Having shown in the last Chapter that, as the appearances of
Final Causes prove an Intelligent *Maker* of the World, so the
particular instances of Final Causes, there mentioned, prove
an Intelligent *Governor* of it. In this Chapter, it is shown
that He is a MORAL *Governor*. Omitting to consider that
the natural notion we have of God is as a Moral Governor,
and that, from the Nature He has given us, we may conclude
that Vice will finally be punished, and Virtue rewarded—
and not dwelling on the proof that, even in this Life, Virtue
has its own reward, and Vice its punishment, it is shown that
the Government by Rewards and Punishments is to be moral.

I. Because no other seems so suited to our minds.

II. Our Prudence is here rewarded, and Imprudence punished

III. Vicious Actions, as injurious to Society, are, in a great
degree, punished.

IV. Virtue, as such, is actually rewarded, and Vice punished :
1st, by their effect on the Mind ; 2d, by the opinion of the
World in general.

V. The natural tendency of Virtue and Vice, if not so much
obstructed, is to produce good and bad effects in a greater
degree than they do ; and it is probable that these Obstruc-
tions will be removed in a Future State.

I. HAVING seen that we are under a government
of rewards and punishments in this life, we shall
next inquire whether this government be *moral*, and,
if so, to what extent ? For *moral* government con-

sists, not barely in rewarding and punishing men for their actions, which the most tyrannical person may do, but in rewarding the righteous and punishing the wicked—in rendering to men according to their actions, considered as good or evil. And the *perfection* of moral government consists in doing this, with regard to all intelligent creatures, in an exact proportion to their personal merits or demerits. Let us, then, examine whether there be in the constitution and conduct of the world any intimations of a moral government—clear to those who will carefully examine it*—and consequently of a Moral Governor. That simple absolute benevolence is the only character and principle of action of the Author of nature—which makes him disregard the actions of his creatures farther than they might produce higher degrees of happiness—requires to be proved before it is asserted. But the possibility of its being proved or disproved is foreign to our purpose, which is to inqnire whether in *our* world a

---

* The objections against religion, from the evidence of it not being universal, nor so strong as might possibly have been, may be urged against natural religion as well as against revealed. And, therefore, the consideration of them belongs to the first part of this treatise as well as the second; but, as these objections are chiefly urged against revealed religion, I chose to consider them in the second part. And the answer to them there (Chap VI.), as urged against Christianity, being almost equally applicable to them as urged against the religion of nature : to avoid repetition, the reader is referred to that chapter.—*Butler*.

E

righteous government be not discernible, which implies necessarily a righteous Governor. It may at once be granted, that, if there be a moral government here, it is not perfect; the question is, therefore, reduced to this, can there be discerned any *principles* of a moral government, further than the moral nature which God has given us, and our natural notion of Him as a Moral Governor?

It might be urged that, in general, less uneasiness and more satisfaction are the natural consequences of a virtuous than of a vicious course of life; but it is difficult so to weigh pleasures and uneasinesses as exactly to estimate the overplus of happiness on the side of virtue; this is more difficult in the case of those who have led a vicious life for some time. *They* have, upon their reformation, their former passions craving for their accustomed gratification; their former vices will be more frequently thrown in their way, by the conversation of men, or otherwise, after their amendment, when, from having acquired a deeper sense of shame, the infamy will be more felt; for, though this properly belongs to their former vices, yet it will, in part, be attributed to their change of life. We, therefore, rather dwell on the following considerations:

Since it has appeared that we are under the government of God, by the methods of rewards and punishments, according to some settled rule of distribution, what rule for finally rewarding and punishing appears more *natural* to us than that of distributing justice ?

II. In this world our prudence is rewarded, and our imprudence punished; the one by satisfaction and external advantages, the other by inconveniences and sufferings. These afford *instances* of a right constitution of nature.

III. Vicious actions are, to a great degree, punished, as mischievous to society, by the actual infliction of the punishment, or by the fear of it. And this is necessary for the very being of society; therefore these punishments are as natural as society itself.

OBJECTION. Actions beneficial to society are often punished, as in the case of persecutions, &c., and actions injurious to it rewarded.

ANSWER. This is not, in the same sense, necessary, and, therefore, not natural, neither are they punished *as being beneficial*, nor rewarded *as being mischievous*.

IV. Virtue, *as such*, is actually rewarded, and vice, *as such*, punished. In order to see this more clearly, we must distinguish between actions *in the abstract*, and with *morality* attached to them. An action by which any natural passion is gratified, or fortune acquired, procures delight or advantages abstracted from all consideration of the morality of such action. Consequently the pleasure or advantage in this case is gained by the action itself—

not by the morality, the virtuousness, or the vi
ciousness of it; though it be, perhaps, virtuous or
vicious. 1st. Then it appears, from the effects of
virtue and vice on the mind and temper, that un
easiness arises from vice—pleasure from virtue
This is evident from daily experience. A man
says, *he is vexed with himself,* when the uneasiness
does not arise from a sense of mere loss or harm,
but from a sense of some action being vicious in a
greater or less degree. This feeling, in more se
rious language, we call *remorse.* Again, a man la
ments an accident or event, and, besides that, feels
additional grief, when he has to admit *that it was
his own doing;* or else some redeeming *satisfaction,*
if he *can not blame himself.* Thus also vice, even
where there is no reason to fear resentment or
shame, causes disturbance from a sense of being
blameworthy. And it may be added—where there
are some fears, not to be got rid of, of the possibil
ity of retribution in after life. On the contrary,
satisfaction and complaisancy are found in the real
exercise of virtue, together with the peaceful hopes
of a better life. 2d. From the opinion of the
world in general—from the encouragement given
by good and honest men, and even by most men, to
a person considered to be virtuous. Public hon
ors are the consequences of actions considered as
virtuous—for example, patriotism, eminent justice;
while actions considered as vicious have been pun-

ished; *e. g.*, tyranny, from a sense of its own nature, independent of the miseries it brings with it. For men resent injuries under the notion, not merely of having received harm, but for having received wrong, and they feel this resentment in behalf of others as well as of themselves. In returning kind actions, we are influenced, not only by the actions themselves, but by the kind intention and good desert they imply in the doer. In *domestic* government, children are punished for falsehood, injustice, &c., as such, and rewarded for the contrary. The authors of crimes, punished by *civil* government, merely as being prejudicial to society, are brought to justice very much from the sense which men have for their actions *as immoral.* Absence or aggravation of guilt in the moral senses often effects the remission or retention of penalties annexed to civil crimes. These instances may seem trivial, but they borrow importance from the subject to which they are applied. But whence is it that virtue, *as such,* is often rewarded, and vice, *as such,* punished, and this rule never inverted ? It proceeds, in part, from the moral nature which God has given us* (and is an *additional* proof to

---

* That we have an approving and disapproving faculty of this kind is evident from our own experience—from the words right and wrong, odious and amiable, base and worthy, with many others of like signification in all languages applied to actions and characters—from the many written systems of morals which suppose it—from our natural sense

that furnished by the possession of such a nature;
for this last is a proof that he will *finally* favor and
support virtue effectually; while the former is an
example of his favoring and supporting it at *present*, at least in some degree), and it proceeds, in
part, from his having given us, together with this
nature, so great a power over each other's happiness and misery.   For, from the first, we are so
made, that well-doing, as such, gives us satisfaction, at least, in some instances—ill-doing, *as such*,
in none.   And, from both conjoined, vice must be,
in some degree, infamous, and men disposed to
punish it, as detestable.   There is nothing on the
side of vice to answer this, because there is nothing
in the human mind contradictory, as the logicians
say, to virtue.   Any instances of such a thing, if
they be not imaginary, are, at least, unnatural perversions.   There are, it is admitted, cases where
persons are prosperous, though wicked—afflicted,
though righteous—and even rewarded for wicked
actions, and punished for virtuous ones.   But this
arises not from the reversion of the natural tendencies of virtue and vice, which is impossible, but
it may arise from there being other wise rules for
the distribution of happiness, besides that of personal merit or demerit, as, for example, the way of

of gratitude, which implies a distinction between merely being the instrument of good and intending it, &c., &c.—*Vide
Bishop Butler on the Nature of Virtue.*

mere discipline. We see enough to know on which side the Author of nature is ; and, in the degree that we co-operate with Him, we naturally feel a secret satisfaction and sense of security, and an implicit hope of somewhat farther ; and this hope is confirmed by—

V. The natural tendency in virtue and vice to produce the good and bad effects now mentioned, in a greater degree than they do, in fact, produce them. For instance, good and bad men would be much more rewarded and punished, *as such*, were it not that justice is often artificially eluded. With regard to *individuals*, these tendencies are obvious. But it may require more particularly to be considered, that power in a *society*, by being *under the direction of virtue*, naturally increases, and has a natural tendency to prevail over opposite power not under the direction of it ; in like manner as power, by being *under the direction of reason*, increases, and has a tendency to prevail over brute force. The superiority which reason gives to power is considered to be, not the accidental, but the natural tendency of reason ; and yet it could not prevail over altogether disproportionate force. It is possible that brute force, either by excess of numbers, by union, by want of sufficient length of time, or of some other opportunities in the rational creatures, should gain the superiority over them. No one would, notwithstanding, hesitate to consider this as an inverted order of things ; *i. e.*, that the *natural* tendency of reason is—to be superior.   Now, *virtue* in a society has a like tendency to procure superiority and *additional power*, considered either as the means of security from opposite power, or of obtaining other advantages.   It has this tendency, among other ways, by rendering public good an object and end to every member of society, and by uniting society by the chief bonds of union—veracity and justice.   But yet there must be some proportion between the natural power or force which *is* under the direction of virtue, and that which *is not :* there must be sufficient length of time ; for the complete success of virtue, as of reason, can not, from the nature of the thing, be otherwise than gradual.   There must be a fair field of trial, a stage large and extensive, proper opportunities for the virtuous to join together, to exert themselves against lawless force, and to reap the fruit of their united labors. Since much less power, under the direction of virtue, would prevail against power not under the direction of it, good men, if united, would prevail even here, to a considerable degree, over the bad. But there are various obstacles to their being united ; for example, they can not be sufficiently assured of each other's characters.   These obstacles may be removed in a future state (which implies a more perfect one, like the state of mature age compared with that of childhood), where men may unite among themselves and with other orders of virtuous creatures. Virtue is here militant. Among other things, the shortness of life denies to it its full scope in several other respects. In a future state it may prevail, and enjoy its consequent rewards. There may be scenes there lasting enough, and, in every other way adapted to afford it a sufficient sphere of action; and it may be added, if this tendency were carried into effect, it would serve as an *example* to those orders of creatures capable of being recovered to a just sense of virtue. These are merely *suppositions*, which are not to be considered true, because not incredible; but they are mentioned to show that there can be no objections against the natural tendency of virtue, from the obstacles that prevent it in this world, as we can easily conceive how these obstacles can be removed; and the presumption that they will be removed, as they are only accidental, is proportionate in degree to the length of time through which the natural tendency will continue. The happy tendency of virtue might be seen by imagining an instance even in this world, by supposing a kingdom, or society of men, perfectly virtuous for a succession of many years—every individual contributing to its preservation by contentedly employing his capacity in its proper sphere; injustice, whether by fraud or force, would be unknown among themselves, and their wisdom, inviolable union, &c., would fully secure them against their neighbors, devoid of such virtuous qualities, allowing both a sufficient time to try their force.   The head of this society, by the tendency and example of virtue, would, in time, become a universal monarch in another sense than any mortal has yet been, and *all people, nations, and languages would serve him.*   And thus the wonderful power and prosperity promised, in Scripture, to the Jews, would be, in a great measure, the *consequence* of what is also predicted of them—" that the *people should be all righteous and inherit the land forever ;*" i. e., taking the term " forever" to mean length of time sufficient to acquire this power.   Suppose the obstacles against the fulfillment of this prediction to be removed, and the dominion and pre-eminence promised must naturally follow to a very considerable degree.   All this might appear of little importance, if we did not consider what would be the consequence if *vice* had naturally those advantageous tendencies, or virtue the direct *contrary* ones.

OBJECTION.   But *prove* that the obstacles will be removed in a future state.

ANSWER.   Even if they were not removed in a future state, if there was to be a continuation of the apparent confusion of rewards and punishments that exists in this, it could not be said that vice, upon the whole, would have the advantage rather than virtue.   But that the future state is to be one perfectly moral, can be proved by the usual arguments, of which the things here alleged afford a strong confirmation ; for, 1st, they show that the Author of nature is not indifferent to virtue and vice, so that even the course of nature, as here explained, furnishes us with a real practical proof of the obligations of religion. 2d. The distributive justice, which Scripture declares is to take place in a future state, will not be different in *kind*, but only in *degree*, from what we experience here : it will be that in *effect* to which we now see a *tendency*. 3d. Our experience that virtue and vice are actually rewarded and punished at present in a certain degree, gives us just ground to hope and to fear that they *may* be rewarded and punished in a higher hereafter ; and 4thly, there is sufficient ground to think that they will, from the natural tendencies of virtue and vice—obstructed, indeed, in this life by obstacles, which being, in numberless cases, only *accidental*, are more likely to be removed in a future state than the *natural* and *necessary* tendencies.

From these things joined with the moral nature which God has given us, considered as given us by Him, arises a practical proof (*vide* chap. 6., *ad fin.*) that it will be completed—a proof from fact, and, therefore, a distinct one from that which is deduced from the eternal and unalterable relations, the fitness and unfitness of actions.*

* *Vide* the Note, Part II., Chap. VIII., 2.

QUESTIONS—CHAPTER III.

1. Explain the meaning of the term "Moral Government," and show in what it consists.

2. In commencing the inquiry "whether in *our* world a righteous government be not discernible," what considerations, that *might fairly* be adduced in proof of it, does Butler omit to press as arguments? What reasons does he give for these omissions?

3. State the *four* general heads, under which the arguments, showing that God's government is to be moral, are comprehended in this chapter.

4. How does it appear from their effects on the *mind* and *temper*, that the uneasiness arises from vice, and pleasure from virtue?

5. Show that from the world in general, virtue, *considered as such*, is actually rewarded; and vice, *considered as such*, punished.

6. Whence is it that the above-mentioned rule of judging and acting is never inverted by *mankind in general* ?

7. To the proof of what assertions does Butler apply these two facts; viz., that mankind *possess a moral nature*, and that they (taken as a whole) judge and act according to it?

8. How may we answer the objection "that some persons are even rewarded for wicked actions, others punished for virtuous ones?"

F

9. Give a summary of the comparison which Butler institutes between *reason* and virtue ; as to their
natural tendency in causing power *under their direction to increase* in a society.

10. Name some of the obstacles which counteract
the natural tendency of virtue to prevail.   How and
when does Butler suppose they may be removed ?

11. For what purpose are the above-mentioned *suppositions* brought forward ?

12. By what supposed case (the *possibility* of which,
however, is intimated in Scripture) may the natural
happy tendency of virtue in a society be seen ?

13. All the reasonings here alleged, affording *confirmation* of the usual arguments that the future state
is to be perfectly moral, are summed up under *four*
heads.   Name them distinctly.

F

CHAPTER IV.

OF A STATE OF PROBATION, AS IMPLYING TRIAL, DIFFICULTIES, AND DANGER.

1. Having shown the confirmation which Analogy affords to the Scriptural Doctrine of a righteous distribution of Rewards and Punishments in a Future State, it is next shown that this World is our state of Probation previous to it. 1st. As implying Trials and Difficulties. 2d. As intended for Moral Discipline and Improvement. 3d. As a Theatre of Action for the manifestation of Persons' Characters to the Creation of God. That this World is a state of Probation in the first sense of the word, is proved in the present Chapter, from the Analogy that, in our *Temporal* Capacity, we are in a state of trial and danger for our *Temporal* Interest.

II. This Analogy is more perfect, since the same constitutes both trials; men behave the same way under them, and the dangers in both are increased from the same causes.

III. Objections answered.

I. A STATE of probation (in the most common meaning of the word) is, in a great measure, the same with the moral government which we have already proved to exist—affording us scopes and opportunities for that good and bad behavior, which God will hereafter reward and punish; for, in order that there may be some ground for future judgment, there must be some sort of temptation to what is wrong ; but the word " probation" expresses more clearly and particularly this allurement to wrong, together with the dangers and difficulties to be encountered in adhering uniformly to what is right.   That the present is such a state appears from the following analogy :—*Natural* government by rewards and punishments, which leaves our happiness and misery dependent on ourselves (chap. 2), as much implies *natural* trial, as *moral* government does *moral* trial.   Accordingly, in our *temporal* interests, we find ourselves in a state of trial ; all temptations to vices contrary to that interest prove it ; also all difficulties and dangers of miscarrying in any thing relating to our worldly happiness.

II. This will more distinctly appear, if we consider, 1st, that the same constitutes both trials ; namely, something either in our external circumstances or in our nature.   In the one case, a temptation may be so singular or sudden as to overpower ; in the other, a person may be so habituated to vice as to seek opportunities, and go out of his way to gratify sinful passions ; and these passions are as much temptations to act contrary to *prudence*, or that reasonable self-love, the end of which is our worldly interest, as they are to act contrary to the principle of *virtue* and *religion*.   However, these

two sources of temptation coincide and mutually
imply each other, for there must be somewhat
within men themselves to render outward circumstances temptations, and there must be external
occasions and exciting objects to render their inward passions so.   Thus mankind, having a temporal interest depending upon themselves, and a
prudent course of behavior being necessary to secure it, passions inordinately excited are dangerous
temptations to forego what is, upon the whole, our
temporal interest, for the sake of present gratification.   Such is our state of trial in our *temporal* capacity ; and it will answer that in our *religious* capacity, by merely substituting the word *future* for
temporal, and *virtue* for *prudence*,* so analogous
are they to each other.   2d. That mankind behave
in the same way under both trials.   Many do not
look beyond their present gratification, not even to
the consequences in this life, whether they are
blinded by inordinate passions, or forcibly carried
away by them against their better judgment, or
willingly yield in defiance of all consequences temporal and eternal.   3d. That the difficulties of
right behavior are increased in a like way in both

---

* Parables are founded on analogical reasoning. *Vide*, in
this case, the Scripture parable of the Ten Virgins, but more
especially that of the Unjust Steward.   "The Lord com-
mended the unjust steward, because he had done wisely, for
the *children of this world are, in their generation, wiser than
the children of light.*"—*Luke*, xvi., 8.

capacities—in our *religious* capacity by the ill behavior of *others*, by an education wrong in a moral
sense, sometimes positively vicious, by general bad
example, by dishonest artifices in business, and by
religious being corrupted into superstitions which
indulge men in their vices. In our *temporal* capacity our difficulties are, in like manner, increased
by a foolish education—by the extravagant and
careless example of others—by mistaken notions,
taken from common opinion, concerning temporal
happiness; and these difficulties are increased to
men, in both capacities, by *their own* wrong behavior in any stage of their existence; for example,
in youth, it renders their stage of trial more dangerous in mature age.

III. 1st Objection. Why is not this state of
trial less uncertain? Would it not be more credible if it were not so uncertain?

Answer. There are natural appearances of our
being in a state of degradation, and, though our
condition *may not appear* the most advantageous,
this furnishes no cause for complaint; for, as men,
by prudent management, can secure, to a tolerable
degree, their temporal interest, so religion requires
no more of us than what we are well able to do, if
we do not neglect the appointed means. But the
chief answer to the objection against such a state
as religion declares this to be, is the foregoing analogy, for, from it, this appears to be throughout

F*

uniform and of a piece with the general conduct
of Providence toward us in all other respects within the compass of our knowledge.   If our *present*
interest were *not* uncertain, but secure, it might
furnish some presumption *against* the truth of religion, which represents our future interest, not as
secure, but depending on our behavior; but from
the contrary being *the fact*, the objection is of no
force.

2d OBJECTION. It is improbable that any kind of
hazard and danger should be put upon us by an
Infinite Being, when every thing which is hazard
and danger in *our* manner of conception, and which
will end in error, confusion, and misery, is now already certain in His foreknowledge.

ANSWER. It might seem improbable, did not
analogy prove it false in fact.   The difficulty of
accounting for it in speculation can not be removed
till we know the whole, or, at least, much more of
the case.

QUESTIONS—CHAPTER IV.

1. What is the meaning of the term, " a state of probation," as used in this work?

2. From what analogy does the present life appear to be such a state?

3. Explain the analogy which appears to exist between our state of trial in our *temporal,* and that in our *religious* capacity.

4. How do mankind commonly behave under both trials?

5. By what causes, common to both, are the difficulties of doing well increased?

6. Answer the following two objections: 1st. Why is not this state of trial less uncertain?

7. 2d Objection. Is it not improbable that *hazard* should be put upon us by a Being whose *foreknowledge* is *certain?*

CHAPTER V.

OF A STATE OF PROBATION, AS INTENDED FOR MORAL DISCIPLINE AND IMPROVEMENT.

1. That we are in a state of Probation, in the second sense, as intended for Moral Discipline and Improvement for another state, appears from Analogy—from the beginning of Life considered as a preparation for mature age.

II. The extent of this Analogy may be determined from the following considerations. 1. In both respects, new Characters must be acquired. 2. We are capable of acquiring these new Characters by our capacities of Knowledge and power of Habit (Habits are either active or passive ; Habits either bodily or mental ; all virtuous Habits formed by active exertion). 3. The possession of these Capacities implies what experience also proves to us—the necessity of using them. And, 4th, we can show how virtuous Habits can be useful in the preparation for another Life ; and Discipline necessary even for Creatures finitely perfect.

III. Objections to such a State answered.

IV. This World is a state of Probation in the third and last sense.

I. FROM considering that we are in a state of probation, the question naturally arises, how came we to be placed in it ? But this is a question involved in insuperable difficulties. We may *lessen* these difficulties by observing that all wickedness is voluntary, and that many of the miseries of life have apparent good effects; but it is plain folly and presumption to pretend to give an account of the whole reason of the matter. Perhaps the discovery or comprehension of it is beyond the reach of our faculties, or, perhaps, the knowledge of it would be prejudicial to us. *Religion* affords a partial answer to it, but a satisfactory one to a question of real importance to us, namely, What is our business here? And this answer is, we are placed in a state of so much affliction and hazard for our improvement in virtue and piety, as the requisite qualification for a future state of security and happiness.

GENERAL ANALOGY: The beginning of life considered as an education for mature age, in the present world, appears plainly to be analogous to this our trial for a future one: the former being in our *temporal* capacity what the latter is in our *religious* capacity. This will more clearly appear from the following:—

II. PARTICULAR ANALOGIES: 1st. Every species of creatures is, we see, designed for a particular way of life, to which the nature, the capacities, temper, and qualifications of each species are as necessary as their external circumstances. One thing is set over against another, as an ancient writer expresses it (Eccles., xlii., 24). Our nature corresponds to our external condition.* So that there must be some determinate capacities—some necessary character and qualifications, without which persons can not but be utterly incapable of a *future* state of life; in like manner as there must be some without which men would be incapable of their present state of life. 2d. The constitution of human creatures, and, indeed, of all creatures within our observation, is such as that they are capable of naturally *becoming qualified* for states of life for which they were once wholly unqualified. We may *imagine* creatures, but we do not know of any, whose faculties are not made for enlargement by experience and habit. We find ourselves in particular, endued with capacities of acquiring knowledge, namely, *apprehension, reason*, and *memory*. And by the *power of habits*, we can acquire a new facility in any kind of action, and settled alterations in our temper and character. But neither the perception of ideas nor knowledge of any sort are habits, though they are absolutely necessary to the forming of them; but the improvements of our

---

* Bishop Butler has clearly shown, in his sermons, the peculiar correspondence between the inward frame of man and the external conditions and circumstances of his life; that the several passions and affections of the heart, compared with those circumstances, are certain instances of final causes; for example, anger leads us to the immediate resistance of injury, and compassion prompts us to relieve the distressed, &c., &c.

capacities of acquiring knowledge, especially in the case of memory, may, perhaps, be so called. That perceptions come into our minds readily and of course, by means of their having been there before, seems a thing of the same kind as readiness in any particular kind of action proceeding from being accustomed to it; and aptness to recollect practical observations of service in our conduct, is plainly habit in many cases. There are habits of perception, as, for example, our constant and even *involuntary* readiness in correcting the impressions of our sight concerning magnitudes and distances, so as to substitute, imperceptibly to ourselves, judgment in the room of sensation. And it seems as if all other associations of ideas, not naturally connected, might be called *passive* habits, as properly as our readiness in *understanding* languages upon sight or *hearing* of words. There are also *active* habits, as, for example, our readiness in *speaking* and *writing* languages. For distinctness, we may consider habits as belonging to the mind or to the body. As habits of the body, *i. e.*, all bodily activities and motions, are produced by exercise; so are habits of the mind—including, under this denomination, general habits of life and conduct, such as those of obedience and submission to authority, or to any particular person; those of veracity, justice, and charity; and those of attention, industry, self-government, revenge. But there is this difference between them, that bodily habits are produced by repeated *external* acts—mental habits by the exertion of *inward* practical principles carried into action, or acted upon.   No *external* course of action can form·*these* habits otherwise than as it proceeds from the inward principles, *e. g.*, of obedience and veracity; because it is only these inward principles *exerted* which are strictly acts of obedience, veracity, &c.   It will contribute toward forming virtuous habits to resolve to do well, and to endeavor to impress on our minds a practical sense of virtue, or to beget in others that practical sense of it which a man really feels himself (for resolutions and endeavors are properly *acts*).   Practical habits are formed and *strengthened* by repeated acts; not so with passive impressions—they *grow weaker* by being repeated; so that going over the theory of virtue in one's thoughts, talking well, and drawing fine pictures, in place of forming a habit of virtue, may form a habit of insensibility to all moral considerations.   Thoughts, by often passing through the mind, are felt less sensibly.   Thus—

(1st.) Being accustomed to danger begets intrepidity, *i. e., lessens* fear.

(2d.) Being accustomed to distress *lessens* the passion of pity.

(3d.) Being accustomed to instances of others' mortality *lessens* the sensible apprehension of our own.

And these effects of active and passive habits may occur at the same time ; active habits may be strengthening while the motives that excite them are less and less sensibly felt ; and experience confirms this, for active principles, at the very time that they are less lively in perception than they were, are found to be somehow wrought more thoroughly into the temper and character, and become more effectual in influencing our practice. Thus, in the three examples of passive habits just mentioned, active habits may be operating at the same time.

(1st.) Active caution may be increasing, while passive fear is growing less.

(2d.) The practical principle of benevolence may be strengthening, while the passive impression of pity, in consequence of *frequently* witnessing distress, will be less and less sensibly felt.

(3d.) It greatly contributes to strengthen a practical regard to death ; *i. e.*, to form a habit of acting with a constant view to it ; to behold daily instances of men dying around us, though these instances give us a less sensible feeling or apprehension of our own mortality.

Thus it appears that *passive* impressions made upon our minds by admonition, experience, and example tend to form active habits, not from our being so affected, but from our being induced to such a course of action ; *i. e.*, it is the acting, and

G

not the affection, that forms them; only it must be
always remembered that real endeavors to enforce
good impressions upon ourselves are a species of
virtuous actions. And practical principles grow
stronger *absolutely* in themselves by exercise, as
well as *relatively* with regard to contrary principles, which, by being accustomed to submit, do so
habitually and of course. Thus a new character,
in several respects, may be formed.

3d. We should be totally unqualified for the
employments and satisfactions of a mature state of
life, unless we exerted the capacities that are *given*
us, and therefore, we may conclude, intended to be
made use of. Even maturity of understanding and
bodily strength require the continued exercise of
our powers of mind and body from our infancy.
But if we suppose a person brought into the world
with both these in maturity, as far as this is conceivable, he would plainly, at first, be as unqualified for the human life of mature age as an idiot.
Want of acquired habits would be like want of
language—it would destroy society. *Children*,
from their very birth, are daily growing acquainted
with the scene in which they are to have a future
part, and learning something necessary to the per-
formance of it; *he*, from his ignorance would be
distracted with astonishment, apprehension, and
suspense. The subordination to which *they* are accustomed teaches them subjection and obedience;

he would be so strangely headstrong and self-willed as to render society insupportable. And there are numberless little rules of action, learned so insensibly as to be mistaken for instinct, which he would be ignorant of, without which we could not live. Thus, by example, instruction and self-government, we are suited to different stations in life, and our conduct in each (which depends upon habits from our youth) determines our character and rank in society. All this is an analogy applicable to the present life, considered as a preparation for a future. Our condition in both respects is uniform, and comprehended under one and the same general law of nature.

4th. But do we know how this world is calculated for such a preparation? If we did not, this would be no objection against it being so. We might, with as much reason, object to the known *fact* that food and sleep contribute to the growth of the body, because we do not know how they can do it, and, prior to experience, we could not have thought that they would. Children are as ignorant that sports and exercise are useful for their health; and they might as well object to restraints in them, and in other matters necessary for their discipline, because they do not see the reason of them. But taking in the consideration of God's moral government, and, consequently, that the character of virtue and piety is a necessary qualification for a future state, we may distinctly see how and in what respects the present life may be a preparation for it, *since we want, and are capable of, improvement in that character by moral and religious habits, and the present life is fit to be a state of discipline for such improvement.* Now, first, as regards the state for which we are to prepare, analogy leads us to conclude that it will be a society as Scripture describes it; and it is not at all unreasonable to suppose, though there be no analogy for it, that it will be, according to the representation of Scripture, under the more immediate or sensible government of God. That we are *capable* of improvement, has been already shown; and that we *want* it, every one will admit who is acquainted with the great wickedness of mankind, or even with those imperfections which the best are conscious of. But the necessity for discipline in human creatures is to be traced up higher than to excess in the passions by indulgence and habits of vice. From the very constitution of their nature they are deficient, and in danger of deviating from what is right, and, therefore, they stand in need of virtuous habits for a security against this danger; for, besides the general principle of moral understanding, they have, in their inward frame, various affections toward external objects, which the principle of virtue can neither excite nor prevent being excited; and when the object of any affection can not be obtained *with* the consent of the moral principle, yet may be obtained *without* it, such affection, though its being excited, and its continuing some time in the mind, be as innocent as it is natural and necessary, tends to incline them to venture upon an unlawful means of indulgence. Now, what is the general security against their actually deviating from what is right? As the danger is from within, so, also, must the security be—from the inward practical principle of virtue ;* and the strengthening this principle will lessen the danger or increase the security against it. All this is under the supposition that particular affections remain in a future state. If this suppo-

* It may be thought that a sense of interest would as effectually restrain creatures from doing wrong. But if, by a *sense of interest*, is meant a speculative conviction, or belief, that such and such indulgence would occasion them greater uneasiness, upon the whole, than satisfaction, it is contrary to present experience to say, that this sense of interest is sufficient to restrain them from thus indulging themselves. And if, by a *sense of interest*, is meant a practical regard to what is, upon the whole, our happiness, this is not only coincident with the principle of virtue or moral rectitude, but is a part of the idea itself. And it is evident this reasonable self-love wants to be improved as really as any principle in our nature; for we daily see it overmatched not only by the more boisterous passions, but by curiosity, shame, love of imitation—by any thing, even indolence; especially if the interest—the *temporal* interest suppose—which is the end of such self-love, be at a distance; so greatly are profligate men mistaken when they affirm they are wholly governed by interestedness and self-love; and so little cause is there for moralists to disclaim this principle.—*Butler.*

G*

sition be true, acquired habits will probably be necessary to regulate them ; if it be not, it amounts to the same thing ; for habits of virtue, thus acquired by discipline, are improvements in *virtue ;* and improvements in virtue must be advancement in *happiness*, if the government of the universe be moral. The necessity of moral improvement by discipline will further appear by considering, 1st, how creatures, made upright, may fall ; and, 2d, how, by preserving their integrity, they may raise themselves to a more secure state of virtue. The nature of liberty can no more account for the former than the possibility of an event can account for its occurrence. But it seems distinctly conceivable, from the very nature of particular affections or propensions ; for, suppose creatures intended for a state of life for which these propensions are necessary, endued with them, together with a moral understanding, having all these principles exactly proportioned to their intended state of life, such creatures would be made upright or finitely perfect. Now, these propensions must be felt, the objects being present ; they can be gratified without the consent of the moral principle, and, therefore, possess some tendency to induce persons to such forbidden gratification ; which tendency, in such particular cases, may be increased by a greater frequency of occasions to excite them, by the least voluntary indulgence, even in thought, till, by peculiar conjunctures conspiring, the *danger* of deviating from right ends in actual deviation—a danger necessarily arising from the very nature of propension, which, on this account, could not have been prevented, though it might have been innocently passed through.* It is impossible to say how far the *first act*† of irregularity might disorder the inward constitution, but *repetition* of irregularity would produce habits; and, in proportion to this repetition, creatures, made upright, would become depraved. But, 2d, by steadily following the moral principle, creatures might have preserved their uprightness, and, consequently, might have been raised to a higher and more secure state of virtue, since the moral principle would gain strength by exercise, and the propensions from habit would more easily submit. Thus, then, vicious indulgence is not only criminal in itself, but also depraves the inward constitution and character. And virtuous self-government is not only right in itself, but also improves the inward constitution, and may improve it to such a degree as that the danger of actually

---

* This proves that it was not necessary for our Lord to take upon him our sinful nature in order to be capable of temptation. *Vide* two Sermons, by Dr. O'Brien, to prove that he might be " tempted *like as we are*, and yet without sin."

† This may serve as an answer to the common objection, that the consequences of a single crime in our first parents are represented in Scripture as incredibly excessive.

deviating from right may be almost infinitely lessened.   Thus it appears, that creatures without
blemish, even possessed of a moral principle, may
be in danger of going wrong, and so stand in need
of the higher perfection and security of virtuous
habits formed in a state of discipline.   Much more
are *they* in danger, and much do *they* require such
habits, whose natures are corrupted, and whose
passions have become excessive from habits of indulgence.   They require to be *renewed*, not merely
improved; for them, discipline of the severer sort
must be necessary.   This world is peculiarly fit to
be a state of discipline for this purpose.   Such experience as it affords of the frailty of our nature—
of the danger and actual event of creatures losing
their innocence and happiness—hath a tendency to
give us a practical sense of things very different
from a *speculative* knowledge of what we are liable
to.   But what renders it peculiarly fit, are the snares
and temptations to vice, because they render caution, recollection, and self-denial necessary to such
as will preserve their integrity.   And strong temptations particularly call these into action; and, requiring a stronger effort of virtue, or a continued
exercising of it, they confirm a habit of it much
more than weak or instantaneous temptations could
possibly do.   It is, indeed, ridiculous to assert that
self-denial is essential to virtue and piety; but it is
nearer the truth, though not strictly the truth itself,

to say, that it is essential to discipline and improvement; for, though actions materially virtuous may not be an exercise of the virtuous principle, *i. e.*, not virtuous actions at all, but merely done from being agreeable to our own particular inclinations, yet they *may* be an exercise of that principle, and, when they are, they tend to form and fix the habit of virtue; and this in proportion to the frequency or intensity of the exercise of the virtuous principle; but, as neither our intellectual power nor bodily strength can be improved beyond a certain degree, and both may be overwrought, possibly there may be some trifling analogy to this in the moral character. Thus it appears, *in general* (for there may be some other minute exceptions), that this world is peculiarly fit to be a state of trial, in the same sense that some sciences are fit to form to habits of attention the minds of *such as will attend to them.* These several observations, concerning the *active* principle of virtue, are applicable to passive submission, or resignation to the Divine will, which is another essential part of a right character, connected with the former, and very much in our power to form ourselves to.

III. 1st OBJECTION. "The present state is so far from proving, in event, a discipline of virtue to the generality of men, that, on the contrary, they seem to make it a discipline of vice."

ANSWER. The viciousness of the world is, in different ways, the great temptation, which renders it a state of virtuous discipline, in the degree it is, to good men. The whole end of man being placed in such a state as the present, is not pretended to be accounted for. It is a discipline to some who attend to and follow the notices of virtue and religion; and if it be not to the generality, this can no more be urged as a proof against its being intended for moral discipline than the decay of the greater part of the numerous seeds of vegetables and bodies of animals put in a way to improve to maturity and perfection can be urged as an objection against their being intended for that end, to which only one in a million attains to.*

2d Objection. As far as a course of behavior materially virtuous proceeds from hope and fear, so far it is only a discipline and strengthening of self-love.

Answer. Doing what God commands, because he commands it, is obedience, though it proceeds from hope or fear; and a course of such obedience will form habits of it. There is no foundation for this great nicety; for veracity, justice, and charity (regard to which must form habits of self-govern-

---

* I can not forbear adding, though it is not to the present purpose, that the *appearance* of such an amazing *waste* in nature, with respect to these seeds and bodies, by foreign causes, is to us as unaccountable as, what is much more terrible, the present and future ruin of so many moral agents by themselves, i. e., by vice.—*Butler.*

ment), respect to God's authority, and to our own chief interest, are not only all three coincident, but each of them is, in itself, a just and natural principle of action.*

3d OBJECTION. How can passive submission and resignation† be in any way necessary to qualify for a state of perfect happiness, since nothing but *afflictions can give occasion for, or require this virtue?*

ANSWER. Experience contradicts this assertion. Even *prosperity* begets extravagant and unbounded thoughts. Imagination is as much a source of discontent as any thing in our external condition. It is, indeed, true, that there can be no scope for patience when sorrow shall be no more; but there may be need of a temper of mind which shall have been formed by patience. For, though self-love, considered as an active principle leading us to pursue our real and chief interest, must coincide with the principle of obedience to God's command (this obedience and the pursuit of our own interest be-

---

* Religion is so far from disowning the principle of self-love, that it often addresses itself to that very principle, and always to the mind in that state where reason presides; and there can no access be had to the understanding but by convincing men that the course of life we should persuade them to is not contrary to their interest.—*Butler's Sermons.*

† Resignation to the will of God is the *whole of piety;* it includes in it all that is good, and is a source of the most settled quiet and composure of mind. It may be said to be perfect when our will is lost and resolved into His.—*Butler's Sermons.*

ing synonymous), yet it can not be said so certainly to coincide, considered merely as the *desire* of our own interest, any more than particular affections can, *i. e.*, so as to be incapable of unlawful excitements. So that *habits* of resignation may, upon this account, be requisite for all creatures—habits, *i. e.*, what are formed by use. However, in general it is obvious that both self-love and particular affections in human creatures, considered only as *passive* feelings, distort and rend the mind, and, therefore, require discipline to moderate them. But the proper discipline for resignation is affliction, since a right behavior under that trial will habituate the mind to a dutiful submission, which, with the active principle of obedience, make up the character which belongs to us as dependent creatures.

4th OBJECTION. All the trouble and danger, unavoidably accompanying such discipline, might have been saved us by our being made *at once* the creatures which we were to be.

ANSWER. This is contrary to the general conduct of *nature*, which is not to save us trouble or danger, but to furnish us with capacities for going through them, and to oblige us to do so. Acquirements of our own experience and habits are the natural supply to our deficiencies, since it is as plainly *natural* to set ourselves to acquire the qualifications as the external things which we stand in need of.

IV. There is a third sense of the word probation : a theatre of action for the manifestation of persons' characters to the creation of God.   This may, perhaps, be only a consequence of our being in a state of probation in the other senses.   However, this manifestation of the real character of men may have respect to a future life in ways unknown to us ; particularly it may be a means of their being disposed of suitably to their characters, and of its being made known to the creation, by way of example, that they are thus disposed of.

H

QUESTIONS—CHAPTER V.

1. What is the only question of *real* importance to us, that arises from the consideration of our being in a state of probation here? And how may it be answered?

2. State, 1st, the general analogy by which Butler illustrates this subject; and, 2d, the four distinct considerations by which he shows the extent and force of that analogy.

3. How does he explain the passage in Ecclesiasticus, chap. xlii., 24; and what consequence does he deduce from it?

4. State what are our capacities of acquiring knowledge; and by what power we may acquire settled alterations of our character.

5. What comparison may we institute between the habits of the *body* and those of the *mind?*

6. Give a summary of the argument showing the *momentous difference* between *practical habits* and *passive impressions* on the mind; noting especially the only way in which the *latter* can become *useful* to us.

7. Prove that the possession of *capacities* implies the necessity also of using them.

8. By what considerations may we distinctly see how, and in what respects, the present life may be a *preparation* for a future state?

9. Show that, from the very constitution of our nature being deficient, there is a necessity for discipline in human creatures.

10. What meaning does Butler affix to the term "a sense of our interest," when he proves it is perfectly compatible with moral rectitude? State his argument on this point.

11. How does it seem distinctly conceivable, from the very nature of particular affections implanted in them, that creatures, made upright, may fall?

12. How does it appear that upright creatures, by pursuing their integrity, may raise themselves to a more secure state of virtue? What inference is drawn from the two foregoing positions?

13. By what arguments is it proved that "this world is *peculiarly fit* to be a state of discipline for the purpose, not merely of *improving*, but of *renewing* men?

14. Answer the following objections. 1st. The present state becomes to most men a discipline of *vice* instead of *virtue*.

15. 2d. Actions proceeding from *hope* or *fear*, though they *be materially* virtuous, only discipline and strengthen *self-love*.

16. 3d. How can *passive submission* and *resignation*, which are required only *in afflictions* (and they are occasioned by a state of sin), serve to qualify us for perfect happiness and virtue?

17. 4th. Might not all our trouble and danger in this state of discipline have been saved by God making us *at once* the creatures which he intends us finally to be?

18. What purpose may be served by the manifestations of the real character of individuals in this life?

CHAPTER VI.

OF THE OPINION OF NECESSITY CONSIDERED AS INFLUENCING PRACTICE.

I. The proof of the existence of an Intelligent Author of nature, taken for granted in this Treatise, is not affected by the opinion of Universal Necessity. For, 1st, when a Fatalist asserts that every thing is by necessity, he must mean by *an agent*, acting necessarily ; and, 2d, the necessity by which such an agent is supposed to act does not exclude intelligence and design.

II. Neither does the opinion of Universal Necessity affect the system of there being a Moral Governor, or of our being in a state of religion ; for, *if* that opinion can be reconciled with our condition under the present Moral Government, it can be reconciled with that which religion teaches us to expect ; but, in the former case, it is found to be *practically false.*

III. The opinion of Universal Necessity does not affect the practical *proof* of religion, derived from the particular final causes of pleasure and pain annexed to actions, combined with the external evidence of Natural Religion.

I. An objection may be made from universal necessity against the existence of an Intelligent Author of nature, which has been taken for granted throughout this treatise as a thing proved, as it may be supposed that such necessity will account for the origin and preservation of all things. But, in the first place, when it is said by a fatalist that every thing is necessary, and could not possibly have been otherwise, it is to be observed that this necessity does not exclude deliberation, choice, preference, and acting from certain principles and to certain 'ends, because all this every man may every moment be conscious of. So that the assertion that every thing is by necessity of nature is not an answer to the question whether the world came into being as it is, by an Intelligent Agent forming it thus or not ? but to quite another question—whether it came into being in that way and manner which we call *necessarily,* or in that way and manner which we call *freely ?* For, suppose farther, that, in a dispute between a fatalist and one who believed himself a free agent, *a house* was instanced; they would both agree that it was built by an architect; the point of their difference would be, whether he built it necessarily, or freely ? We ascribe to God a necessary existence,* uncaused,

* As to the meaning of *necessary existence,* logicians have long since determined that there are but two modes according to which any Being can be said to exist, or to be what it is; and these are *contingency* and *necessity.* Where the non-existence of a Being is possible, that is, where we can, without a contradiction, suppose it *not to exist,* that Being exists *contingently,* or contingency is the *mode* of its existence. But if there is any Being who demonstrably *must exist,* and whose non-existence is therefore impossible and inconceivable, that

by any agent: for we find within ourselves the idea of infinity, *i. e.*, immensity and eternity, impossible even in imagination to be removed out of being; and from hence (for this *abstract*, as much as any other, implies a *concrete*) we conclude that there is, and can not but be, an Infinite and Immense Eternal Being, answering this idea, existing prior to all design contributing to his ˙existence; and, therefore, from the scantiness of language, we say necessity is the foundation of his existence. But there can not be said to be this kind of necessity for the existence of every thing—a necessity *antecedent in nature to design*, for many reasons: but chiefly because it is admitted that *design* in the actions of men contributes to many alterations in nature.

II. The condition of mankind under the present moral government being greatly analogous to our condition under a farther government, which religion teaches us—*if* any assert, as the fatalist must, that the opinion of universal necessity is reconcilable with the former, there immediately arises a question, in the way of analogy,* whether he must

---

Being exists *necessarily*, or necessity is the *mode* of its existence.   But necessity can in no sense be considered as the cause, or even as the ground or reason of any existence, or of any effect whatever.—*Hamilton on the Existence of God.*

* "Fatalists are fond of inferring moral *necessity* from physical, in the *way of analogy*. In effect, says Voltaire, it would be very singular that all nature, all the planets, should obey

not also own it to be reconcilable with the latter, *i. e.*, with the system of religion itself, and the proof of it.   Suppose, then, a fatalist to educate any one from his youth up in his own principles—to eradicate the very perceptions of blame and commendation out of his mind, by teaching him that he can not possibly behave otherwise than he does; suppose the child to judge, from *this system*, what treatment he is to expect from reasonable men, upon his coming abroad into the world—as the fatalist judges from it what he is to expect from the Author of nature, and with regard to a future state.   At first he would have a great degree of conceit and vanity at being freed from the restraints of fear and shame with which his playfellows were fettered; but this is not all; he must evidently, by constant correction, have the want of those natural perceptions of blame and commendation supplied, which this system destroyed, and thus be convinced that, if it be not eternal laws, and that there should be a little animal five feet high, who, in contempt of these laws, could act as he pleased, solely according to his caprice.   We do too much honor to such reasoning when we reply to it in the bold but sublime words of a great genius:"

> Know'st thou th' importance of a soul immortal?
> Behold this midnight-glory, worlds on worlds!
> Amazing pomp!   Redouble this amaze;
> Ten thousand add; add twice ten thousand more;
> Then weigh the whole.   One soul outweighs them all,
> And calls the astonishing magnificence
> Of unintelligent creation poor.
>
> BEATTIE.

false, it is misapplied when applied to practice.
Or, supposing his temper could remain still formed to the system, upon his coming abroad into
the world he would be insupportable to society,
and the treatment which he would receive from it
would render it so to him; and he could not fail
of soon committing some act for which he would
be delivered over into the hands of civil justice.
Any other *practical* application of this opinion will
be found equally fallacious; for instance, that there
is no need for taking care to preserve life, for, if
we are destined to live, we shall live without it;
and, if to die, we can not prevent it. None of these
practical absurdities result from reasoning upon the
supposition that we are free; and, therefore, though
it were admitted that this opinion of necessity were
speculatively true, yet, with regard to practice, it is
as if it were false, so far as our experience reaches;
that is, to the whole of our present life. And how
can people think themselves so very secure, that
the same application of the same opinion may not
mislead them also, in some analogous manner, with
respect to a future one, on which is dependent a
more general and more important interest ? For
religion being a *practical* subject, and the analogy
of nature showing us that we have not faculties to
apply this opinion, were it a true one, to practical
subjects, whenever we do apply it to the subject
of religion, and thence conclude that we are free

from its obligations, it is plain this conclusion can not be depended upon. Nor does this contain any reflection upon reason, but only upon what is unreasonable—applying our reason to subjects to which experience shows us they are not suited. Farther, we find within ourselves a will, and are conscious of a character, *i. e.*, that frame of mind whereby we act in one manner rather than another. Now, if this in *us* be reconcilable with fate, it is reconcilable with it in the *Author of nature* (besides natural government and final causes imply a character and a will in the Governor concerning the creatures whom He governs); and it is as reconcilable with the *particular* character of benevolence, veracity, and justice in Him, which attributes are the foundation of religion, as with any other character, since we find this necessity no more hinders *men* from being benevolent than cruel—true than faithless—just than unjust—or, if the fatalist pleases, what *we* call unjust. For it is said, indeed, that what, upon supposition of *freedom*, would be just punishment, upon supposition of necessity becomes manifestly unjust; because it is punishment inflicted for doing what persons could not avoid doing. As if the necessity which is supposed to destroy the injustice of murder, for instance, would not also destroy the injustice of punishing it. However, as little to the purpose as this objection is in itself, it shows how the notions of justice and injustice force themselves upon the mind, even while we are making suppositions destructive of them.

III. But, though it is most evident that universal necessity, if it be reconcilable with any thing, is reconcilable with that character in the Author of nature, which is the foundation of religion, yet does it not plainly destroy the *proof* that He is of that character, and consequently the *proof* of religion? By no means; for we find that happiness and misery are not our *fate* in any such sense as not to be the consequences of our behavior, but that they are the *consequences* of it. But as the doctrine of liberty, though experienced to be true, may be perplexed with difficulties, and as necessity seems to be the basis of infidelity, we shall prove more *distinctly* and *particularly* that necessity does not destroy the obligations of religion. The proof, from final causes, of an Intelligent Author of nature, is not affected by it. And it is a matter of *fact*— and, therefore, there can be no objection against it from necessity—that He governs the world by the method of rewards and punishments, and also that He hath given us a moral faculty, by which we distinguish between actions virtuous and vicious. This is a rule of such authority, that we can not depart from it without being self-condemned. It is plainly a Divine command, immediately producing a sense of duty, being a direction of the Author of nature to creatures capable of looking upon it as such; and his having annexed to some actions an inseparable sense* of good desert, and to others of ill, surely amounts to *declaring* upon whom his punishment shall be hereafter inflicted, and his rewards be bestowed.† But besides this, natural religion hath an external evidence which the doctrine of necessity, if it could be true, would not effect. 1st. Somewhat of this system has been professed in all ages and countries of which we have any information. This general consent shows the system to be conformable to the common sense of mankind. 2d. It is a certain historical fact, as far as we can trace, that religion was believed in the first ages of the world, and this when it was unadulterated by superstition. The only alternative is, either that it came into the world by revelation, or that it is natural and obvious, and forces itself upon the mind. The former is the conclusion of

* From hence might easily be deduced the obligation of *religious worship*, were it only to be considered as a means of preserving upon our minds a sense of this moral government of God, and securing our obedience to it; which yet is an extremely imperfect view of that most important duty.— *Butler.*

† The conclusion, that God will finally reward the righteous and punish the wicked, is not here drawn from it appearing to us *fit* that *He should*, but from its appearing that He has told us He *will*. However, I am far from intending to deny that the will of God is determined by what is fit, by the right and reason of the case; though such abstract subjects are rather to be declined, or, at least, treated with caution.—*Butler.*

learned men, rendered more probable by the inaptness of uncultivated minds for speculation, and by the early pretenses to revelation, otherwise not easily accounted for. 3d. There is express historical, or *traditional* evidence, as ancient as history, of the system of religion being taught mankind by revelation; and why should not the most ancient *tradition* be admitted as some additional proof of a fact against which there is no presumption; and this proof is mentioned here, because it tends to show that religion came into the world by revelation prior to all consideration of the proper authority of any book supposed to contain a revelation, and even prior to all consideration whether the revelation itself be purely handed down.

It is carefully to be observed, and ought to be recollected, after all proofs of virtue and religion, which are only general, that, as speculative reason may be neglected, prejudiced, and deceived, so also may our moral understanding be impaired and perverted, and the dictates of it not impartially attended to; this should admonish us not to take custom, and fashion, and slight notions of honor, or imaginations of present ease, use, and convenience to mankind for the only moral rule.

The foregoing observations together amount to a practical proof, sufficient to influence the actions of men, who act upon thought and reflection, if it were admitted that there is no proof of the contrary.

OBJECTION. "There are many probabilities which can not be shown to be no probabilities, and yet may be overbalanced by greater probabilities on the other side; much more by demonstration. And there is no occasion to object against *particular* arguments alleged for an opinion, when the *opinion itself* may be clearly shown to be false. Now the method of government by rewarding and punishing good and ill desert, as such, supposes that we are free, and not necessary, agents; and it is incredible that the Author of nature should govern us upon a supposition, as true, which he knows to be false,* and, therefore, absurd to think that he will reward or punish us for our actions hereafter, especially considered as of good or ill desert."

ANSWER. The whole analogy of nature shows that the conclusion, from this reasoning, is false, wherever the fallacy lies. The doctrine of freedom, indeed, clearly shows where—in supposing ourselves necessary, when, in truth, we are free agents. But, upon supposition of necessity, the fallacy lies in taken for granted that it is incredible

---

* Hume goes so far as to affirm, "that, though man, in truth, is a necessary agent, having all his actions determined by fixed and immutable laws, yet, this being concealed from him, he acts with the conviction of being a free agent." Who conceals it? Does the Author of nature conceal it, and this writer discover it?

> To laugh were want of goodness and of grace,
> And to be grave exceeds all power of face.
>   BEATTIE.

I

that necessary agents should be rewarded and punished. It is matter of fact that men are rewarded and punished for their actions, considered as virtuous and vicious; so that, if it be incredible that necessary agents should be thus rewarded and punished, then men are not necessary, but free. But if, on the contrary—which is the supposition we have been arguing upon—it be insisted that men are necessary agents, then there is nothing incredible in the farther supposition of necessary agents being thus rewarded and punished, since we ourselves are thus dealt with.

Is, then, the common assertion true, that the opinion of necessity is essentially destructive of all religion? It is true, 1st, in a practical sense, that atheists encourage themselves in vice by this notion. 2d. In the strictest sense, that it is contrary to the whole constitution of nature, and so to every thing. But it is not true; as we have seen that necessity, supposed reconcilable with the constitution of things, is not also reconcilable with natural religion; its proof remains unaffected by it, and, therefore, the proof of revealed religion.

QUESTIONS—CHAPTER VI.

1. Show that the proof of the existence of an intelligent Author of nature is not affected by the opinion of universal necessity; and give a familiar illustration of the argument.

2. Explain the meaning of ascribing to God a *necessary existence*. Why can not any thing similar be predicted of all natural objects?

3. In what manner does Hamilton distinguish between the existence of God and creatures?

4. By what examples does Butler illustrate his assertion, that the opinion of universal necessity, when *practically* applied to our condition in the present life, is found to be fallacious?

5. How is it proved that, in the application of the above opinions to the things of a future life, it will be found equally fallacious?

6. Show that from the fact of "our finding within ourselves a *will*, and our being conscious of a certain character belonging to us," arguments may be deduced against the idea of Universal Necessity affecting the system of a Moral Governor.

7. Prove that the opinion of necessity does not affect the practical proof of religion, derived from the particular final causes of pleasure and pain annexed to actions.

8. State the heads under which it is argued, that natural religion has an external evidence that can not be affected by the doctrine of necessity.

9. Answer upon his own grounds the following objection of a fatalist, viz., "the method of government by rewards and punishments in a future life must go upon the supposition that we are *not necessary* agents; but the Author of nature knows that we are so; and, therefore, will not reward or punish us for our actions hereafter under the notion that they are of good or ill desert."

10. In what sense is it true that the doctrine of necessity is essentially destructive of all religion?

CHAPTER VII.

OF THE GOVERNMENT OF GOD CONSIDERED AS A
SCHEME OR CONSTITUTION, IMPERFECTLY COMPRE-
HENDED.

I. Admitting the credibility of the general doctrine of religion as a matter of *fact*, there may yet be objections
against the *wisdom, justice, and goodness* of it. Analogy
affords a general answer to such objections, by showing
that God's moral government must be a *scheme* beyond
our comprehension.

II. This appears more clearly from particular analogies. 1st.
In the natural government means are used to accomplish
ends, and often such means as appear to us unsuitable.
2d. The natural government is carried on by *general*
laws, with which we are unacquainted.

III. Objection answered, viz:—" This is only arguing from
our *ignorance*, which may as well be made use of to invalidate the proof of religion."

I. HAVING shown the credibility of religion, as a
matter of fact, there may yet be objections against
the wisdom, equity, and goodness of the Divine
government implied in the notion of religion, and
against the method by which this government is
conducted. To these objections analogy can fur-

1*

nish no *direct* answer.   For the credibility or certainty of a *matter of fact*, which is all that analogy
can directly prove, does not immediately prove
any thing concerning the wisdom or goodness of
it.   But analogy furnishes a remote answer—it
suggests, and *makes it credible*, that this government must be a scheme or system, as distinguished
from a number of single, unconnected acts of distributive justice and goodness, and a scheme beyond our comprehension.*

GENERAL ANALOGY. Upon supposition that God
exercises a moral government over the world, the
analogy of his natural government suggests and
makes it credible that his moral government must
be a scheme quite beyond our comprehension.—
1st. *It must be a scheme*—for the world, and the
whole natural government of it, appears to be so,
—to be a scheme or system, whose parts corre-
spond to each other, and to a whole, as really as
any work of art, or as any particular model of a
civil constitution and government.   And as there
is not any action or natural event, with which we
are acquainted, so single and unconnected as not to
have a respect to some other actions and events,
so, possibly, each of them, when it has not an im-

---

* The ignorance of man is a favorite doctrine with Bishop
Butler.   It occurs again in the second part of the Analogy;
it makes the subject of his 15th Sermon, and we meet with
it also in his Charge.

mediate natural relation to other actions and events, may yet have a remote one, beyond the compass of this present world. Things, apparently the most inconsiderable, are perpetually observed to be necessary conditions to the most important matters; so that any one thing whatever, for aught we know to the contrary, may be a necessary condition to any other. In short, there is not any one thing of which we can give the whole account, of all its causes, ends, and adjuncts necessary to its existence. Thus it appears that the natural government is a scheme, and a scheme so incomprehensible, that a man must really know nothing at all who is not sensible of his ignorance in it. This immediately suggests, and strongly shows the credibility, that the moral world and government of it may be so too. Indeed, the natural and moral constitution and government are so connected as to make up together but one scheme; and it is highly probable, but more than is necessary to be proved at present, that the first is formed and carried on merely in subserviency to the latter, as the vegetable world is for the natural and organized bodies for minds. In the same way, then, every act of Divine justice and goodness may be supposed to look much beyond itself and its immediate object; it may have some reference to other parts of God's moral administration, and to a general moral plan: and *every circumstance* of this government may be adjusted beforehand, with a view to the whole of it; as, for example, the time, degrees, and ways in which virtue is to remain in a state of warfare and discipline, and in which wickedness is permitted to have its progress; the kinds of rewards and punishments, &c., &c.[*]   And supposing this to be the case, it is most evident that we are not competent judges of this scheme, from the small parts of it which come within our view in the present life, and therefore we are supplied with an answer to all objections to it.   For, suppose it were objected, "the origin and continuance of evil might easily have been prevented by repeated interpositions, so guarded as to preclude all mischief arising from them.   Or, if this were impracticable, that a *scheme* or system of government is itself an imperfection, since more good might have been produced without it, by continued single, unconnected acts of distributive justice and goodness, because these would have occasioned no irregularities."   The answer is obvious.   Were these assertions true, yet the government of the world might be just and true,

* There is no manner of absurdity in supposing a veil, on purpose, drawn over some scenes of infinite power, wisdom, and goodness, the sight of which might, some way or other, strike us too strongly; or that better ends are designed and served by their being concealed than could be by their being exposed to our knowledge.   The Almighty may cast clouds and darkness round about Him for reasons and purposes of which we have not the least glimpse or conception.—*Butler's Sermons.*

notwithstanding; for, at the most, they would infer nothing more than that it might have been better. But, indeed, they are mere arbitrary assertions, no man being sufficiently acquainted with the possibilities of things to bring any proof of them to the lowest degree of probability; for though what is asserted may seem to be possible, yet many instances may be alleged, in things much less out of our reach, of suppositions absolutely impossible, which few would perceive to be such, and perhaps no one, at first sight, suspect.   Some *unknown* relation, or some *unknown* impossibility, may render what is objected against just and good, nay, good in the highest practicable degree.

▉ PARTICULAR ANALOGIES: 1st. As in the scheme of the natural world no ends appear to be accomplished without means, so we find that means very undesirable often conduce to bring about ends, in such a measure desirable, as greatly to overbalance the disagreeableness of the means.   Experience also shows many means to be conducive and necessary to accomplish ends, which means, before experience, we should have thought would have had even a *contrary* tendency.   In the same way, the things objected against in the moral government, may be means by which an overbalance of good, will, in the end, be found produced; and likewise, it appears to be no presumption against this, that we do not see those means to have any such tendency, or that they seem to us to have a contrary one.

In order to obviate an absurd and wicked conclusion from any of these observations, it is to be observed, that though the actual permission of evil may be beneficial to the world (*i. e.*, less mischievous than if it had been forcibly prevented by another person), yet it would have been much more beneficial if this evil had never been done. Thus, in the *natural* world, some disorders bring their own cures—some diseases are themselves remedies. Many a man would have died, had it not been for the gout or a fever; yet it would be thought madness to assert that sickness is a better or more perfect state than health; though the like has been asserted with regard to the *moral* world.

2d. The natural government of the world is carried on by *general* laws. For this there may be wise and good reasons: and that there are such may be concluded from analogy. For we have scarce any kind of enjoyments but what we are, in some way or other, instrumental in procuring ourselves, by acting in a manner which we foresee likely to procure them; now there could not be this foresight were not the government of the world carried on by general laws. Though every *single* case may be at length found to have been provided for, even by these, yet, by general laws, the prevention of all irregularities may be naturally impossible. *Objected.* Could not then the necessary defects of general laws be remedied by interpositions? *Ans.* This were to be wished, if these interpositions would have no other effects; but it is plain they would have some visible and immediate bad effects—for instance, they would encourage idleness and negligence, and they would render doubtful the natural rule of life, which is ascertained by this very thing, that the course of the world is carried on by general laws. And it is certain they would have distant effects, and very great ones too, by means of the wonderful connections before mentioned: thus, for aught we know, interpositions would produce greater evil than they would prevent, and prevent greater good than they would produce; so that the not interposing, so far from being a ground of complaint, is an instance of goodness.

III. Objected against this whole argument from our ignorance. "We must argue from what we know, not from what we are unacquainted with; or, however, the answers here given to *objections* against religion might equally be made use of to invalidate its *proof.*

Answer: 1st. Though *total* ignorance in any matter *equally* precludes all proof concerning it, and objections against it, yet *partial* ignorance does not. The proof of religion is a proof of the **moral character** of God, and consequently that his government is moral.   We may know this, and yet not know the means for accomplishing it ; so that objections against the means actually made use of might be answered by our ignorance—though the proof that such an end was intended might not be at all invalidated by it.   2dly. Admitting that the proof of religion was affected by it, yet it is undeniably true that moral obligations would remain certain ;. for they arise immediately and necessarily from the judgment of our own mind, unless perverted, which we can not violate without being self-condemned ; and the credibility that the consequences which religion teaches us, *may* result, would make them certain from considerations of interest.

But, 3dly, the above *analogies* show that the way of arguing made use of in objecting against religion is delusive, because they show it is not at all incredible, that, could we comprehend the whole, we should find the permission of the disorders objected against to be consistent with justice and goodness, and even instances of them.   Now this is not applicable to the proof of religion, as it is to the objections against it, and therefore can not invalidate that proof, as it does these objections.

4thly. Strictly speaking, as it appears from the last observation, the answers above given are not taken merely from our ignorance, but from somewhat which analogy shows us concerning it.

CONCLUSION.* The credibility of religion, from experience and facts here considered, should afford sufficient motives to religion, and ought to make men live in the general practice of virtue and piety. The plea of ungovernable passion, on the side of vice, is no reason, and is but a sorry excuse ; for men, in their temporal concerns, are inured and necessitated to govern their passions. But the proper motives to religion are the proper proofs of it, from our moral nature,† from the presages of conscience, and from our natural apprehension of God under the character of a righteous Governor and Judge—a nature, conscience, and apprehension

* A connected view of the preceding Part, similar to that in the conclusion of the original, may be formed by reading in continuation the short summaries prefixed to each chapter.

† St. Paul commences his Epistle to the Romans with the professed acknowledgment, or rather the authoritative assertion, of the two great evidences of Natural Religion—the one legible in the book of the Creation, the other indigenous in the soul of man. This latter is the moral *constitution of our souls*, which is the transcript, obscured and defaced indeed, but still the transcript of the great law of God : that law which the very Heathen know, and can not avoid knowing, because " they have the work of it written in their hearts," and their thoughts " accusing or excusing them" by its dictates. And when St. Paul *charges* the Gentiles with the *knowledge* of this law, it is such a knowledge, as in his mind, was sufficient to bring them under the *capacity*, and consequent *obligation*, of some *obedience ;* otherwise his whole doctrine and inculcation of that law, as subjecting them to judgment, would be a lifeless argument.—*Davison on Primitive Sacrifice.*

K

given us by Him; and from the confirmation of
the dictates of reason given us by *life and immortality brought to light by the Gospel;* and *the wrath
of God revealed from heaven, against* all ungodli-
ness and unrighteousness of men.

QUESTIONS—CHAPTER VII.

1. What answer can *analogy* furnish to objections against the wisdom, justice, and goodness of God's moral government?

2. How does it appear that God's *natural* government of the world is a *scheme*, and one that is incomprehensible?

3. To what extent does Butler assert that the Divine, natural, and moral governments are connected; and what does he suppose to be credible from them?

4. Prove that, from our very ignorance of the universal scheme of Divine government, we are supplied with a reasonable answer to all objections against it.

5. "In the scheme of the natural world no ends are accomplished without means; and good ends are often brought about by means *undesirable* and *apparently unsuitable.*" Apply this to the case of the moral world.

6. What good reasons may be given for the fact, that the natural government of the world is carried on by *general* laws?

7. Answer the following objections:

1st. That we must argue from what we know, not from what we are unacquainted with.

8. 2d Objection. That the answers here given to objections against religion might equally be made use of to invalidate its proof.

9. What conclusion does Butler draw from all that he has advanced in respect of natural religion?

SCHEME OF PART II.

OF REVEALED RELIGION.

PART II.

OF REVEALED RELIGION.

CHAPTER I.

OF THE IMPORTANCE OF CHRISTIANITY.

I. The *importance* of Christianity is here considered, as it can not but be a proper introduction to a Treatise concerning the *credibility* of it ; especially as there are some who reject revelation as in its very notion incredible ; and others who think it of indifferent value, as they both consider the light of nature to be sufficient.

II. The importance of Christianity is more distinctly shown by considering it, 1st, As a republication of Natural Religion, being authoritative, with new light, and other circumstances of peculiar advantage. 2d, As containing an account of things not discoverable by reason, in consequence of which several distinct *precepts* are enjoined us.

III. Two deductions are added by way of illustration, stating the distinction between *moral* and *positive* precepts, and the preference due to the former.

K*

I. SOME persons avowedly reject all revelation, as in its very notion incredible, and necessarily fictitious, as the light of nature is considered to be fully sufficient.* Indeed, if it were so, no revelation would have been given. But that it is not, appears from the state of religion in the Heathen world before revelation, and its present state in those countries which have borrowed no light from it—from the doubts of the greatest men concerning vital points, and the inattention and ignorance of mankind in general. It is not likely that *any* could reason out natural religion clear of superstition. Certainly the generality would want the *power*, or the *inclination*. But admitting that they did not, and so might reason it out, revelation might be required, and might afford the greatest assistance and advantage.† Therefore to affirm that revelation is superfluous, is not less extravagant than saying that, men being so completely happy in the present life, it implies a contradiction to suppose they could be more so.

* That the principles of natural religion have come to be so far understood and admitted as they are, may fairly be taken for one of the effects of the Gospel revelation ; *a proof of its actual influence on opinions at least, instead of a disproof of its necessity or use.—Davison on Prophecy.*

† Socrates, Plato, Confucius, and others, the bright and shining lights of antiquity, have given their authority to the opinion of the probability of a revelation from God.—*Vide Leland on the Advantages and Necessity of the Christian Revelation.*

But, 2dly, there are other persons not to be ranked with these, who, with little regard to the evidence of revelation, or even upon the supposition of its truth, affirm that its *only design* must be to establish the moral system of nature, and to enforce the practice of natural piety and virtue; but that it is immaterial whether these things are believed and practiced upon the evidence and motives of nature or of revelation.   Now, this opinion borders very nearly upon the former, and therefore the particular consideration of it will be a confirmation of the answer above given.   At first sight it is evident, if God has given a revelation, we can not consider it an indifferent matter whether we obey or disobey the commands contained in it, unless we are certain that we know *all* the reasons for them, and that they are now ceased; and this is a thing impossible.

II. But the importance of Christianity will more distinctly appear, by considering it, 1st, as a republication and external institution of natural or essential religion; and, 2dly, as containing an account of a dispensation of things not discoverable by reason, in consequence of which several distinct precepts are enjoined us.

1st. It is a republication of natural religion.*

---

* It has been admitted by Infidels, that Christianity is a republication of the law of nature; but they deny that there are any additional advantages arising out of this republication.

It instructs mankind in the moral system of the world—that it is the work of an infinitely perfect Being, and under his government—that virtue is His law, and that there will be a future righteous judgment.   This republication presents natural religion *free from the superstition* under which it was in a manner lost.   It is *authoritative,* and so affords the evidence of testimony for the truth of it. For though the miracles and prophecies recorded in Scripture were intended to prove a *particular* dispensation of Providence, yet they prove God's *general* providence as our moral Governor and Judge;* for these two are necessarily connected, and they are both alike taught by those that wrought the miracles and delivered the prophecies. While the law of Moses, then, and the Gospel of Christ, afford the only evidence of revealed religion, they afford an additional evidence, and a new *practical* proof of natural religion; for would not the working of miracles, and foretelling of future events, add credibility and authority to a person,

So that if they do not themselves draw the conclusion, they leave it to be inferred, that Christianity is useless.   This latter is the method and design of the author of "Christianity as Old as the Creation."

* Miracles not only contain a new demonstration of God's existence, but strengthen the proofs it draws from the frame of the world, and clear them from the two principal objections of Atheism, viz., either that the world is eternal, or that it owed its existence to the fortuitous concourse of atoms.— *Vide Farmer on Miracles.*

e. g., teaching natural religion to a nation wholly ignorant of it ? or would it not be a great confirmation to a person who had never heard of a revelation, believing from principles of reason in the
moral system of things, but yet wavering from perceiving in the world little or no practical sense of
these things, to hear that this system was distinctly
revealed, and that the revelation was proved by
miracles ?   Farther, this is a *clear* republication of
the doctrine of a future state—of the danger of
a course of wickedness, and especially of the efficacy of repentance.   Life and immortality are emi-
nently brought to light by the Gospel.   Moreover,
revelation considered only as subservient to natural
religion, is important as an *external institution* of
it.   As miraculous powers were given to the first
preachers of Christianity, in order to their introducing it into the world, *a visible church* was established, in order to continue it, and carry it on suc-
cessively throughout all ages.   This visible church
is like a city built upon a hill, a standing memorial
to the world of the duty which we owe our Maker
—a repository of the oracles of God.   It prevents
us forgetting the *reality* of religion, by the *form* of
it being ever before our eyes ; and it has a further
tendency to promote natural religion, as being an
instituted method of education, that *the body of
Christ*, as the Scripture speaks, *should be edified*.
The benefit of a visible church being thus apparent,

it follows that positive institutions are beneficial, for the *visibility of the church consists in them.* The importance of Christianity in this view, then, is far from being inconsiderable. It lays every Christian practically under an obligation to contribute toward continuing and carrying it on.* If any one will yet doubt whether there arises from Christianity any benefit to natural religion, let him consider whether the generality of mankind in the Heathen world were in as advantageous a situation with regard to natural religion, as they are now among us?

OBJECTED. Christianity has been perverted, and has had little good influence.

ANSWER. Even admitting this assertion (though the effects of Christianity have been by no means small, nor its supposed ill effects, properly speaking, any effects of it at all),† the dispensations of Providence are not to be judged of by their perversions, but by their genuine tendencies—by what they would effect if mankind performed their duty; for

---

* From these things appears the weakness of all pleas for neglecting the public service of the church. For though a man prays with as much devotion and less interruption at home, and reads better sermons there, yet that will by no means excuse the neglect of his appointed part of keeping up the profession of Christianity among mankind. This neglect, were it universal, must be the dissolution of the whole visible church.—*Bishop Butler's Sermon before the Society for the Propagation of the Gospel.*

† *Vide* Paley's Evidences, Part III., Chap. 7.

such an objection applies with the same force against the manifestation of the law of nature by reason, as we see that has been perverted, and thus it leads to downright Atheism.

2d. But revelation makes known to us, in addition to the general providence of God in natural religion, a particular dispensation of providence carrying on by His Son and Spirit. From this being revealed, important duties arise on our part to the Son and Holy Ghost. We are to be baptized in their name, as well as in the name of the Father. Now, the importance of these duties may be judged of by considering that they arise not merely from positive command, but also from the offices, which appear from Scripture to belong to these Divine Persons in the Gospel dispensation, or from the relations which they are declared to stand in to us. Now, considering religion as divided into internal and external, under the first notion, the essence of natural religion may be said to consist in religious regards to *God the Father Almighty*, and the essence of revealed religion, as distinguished from natural, to consist in religious regards to the *Son and to the Holy Ghost*. And the obligations we are under, of paying these religious regards to each of these Divine Persons respectively, arise from the respective relations which they each stand in to us. How these relations are made known, whether by reason, as those belonging to the first Person are, or

by revelation, as those belonging to the other two
Persons, makes no alteration in the case, because
the duties arise out of the relations themselves, not
out of the manner in which we are informed of them.
The Son and Spirit have each his proper office in
that great dispensation of Providence—the redemption of the world—the one our Mediator, the other
our Sanctifier.   Before revelation, we could be under no obligations from these offices and relations,
yet upon their being revealed, the duty of religious
regards to both these Divine Persons, as immediately arises from them, as charity toward our
fellow-creatures arises out of the common relations
between us and them.   But it will be asked, What
are these inward religious regards ?   I answer, the
religious regards of reverence, honor, love, trust,
gratitude, fear, hope.   In what *external* manner this
inward worship is to be expressed is a matter of
pure revealed command ; as perhaps the external
manner in which God the Father is to be worshipped, may be more so than we are ready to
suppose.

The conclusion from all this is, that Christianity
can never be esteemed of little consequence, till it
be positively supposed false.   If Christ be what
Scripture declares him to be, no one can say what
may follow not only the obstinate, but the careless
disregard of the high relations He stands in to us
as our Lord, our Saviour, and our God.   If we re-

quire the assistance of the Holy Ghost to renew
our nature for another state (as Scripture declares
—" Except a man be born of water and the Spirit, he can not enter into the kingdom of God."—
John, iii., 5), is it a slight matter whether we make
use of the means, expressly commanded by God
for obtaining this Divine assistance, when analogy
shows us that without using the appointed means
we can not expect any benefit? Reason shows us
nothing of the particular immediate means of obtaining either temporal or spiritual benefits. This,
therefore, we must learn, either from *experience* or
revelation. And the present case does not admit
of experience.

III. The two following deductions may be proper to be added, in order to illustrate the foregoing
observations, and to prevent their being mistaken.

First. Hence we may clearly see where lies the
distinction between what is positive, and what is
moral, in religion.

Moral Precepts, are precepts the reasons of
which we see.

Positive Precepts, are precepts the reasons of
which we do not see.*

* This is the distinction between moral and positive precepts, considered respectively as such. But yet, since the
latter have somewhat of a moral nature, we may see the
reason of them considered is this view. Moral and positive
precepts are in some respects alike, in other respects different. So far as they are alike, we discern the reasons of both:

Moral Duties, arise out of the nature of the case itself, prior to external command.

Positive Duties, do not arise out of the nature of the case itself, but from external command: nor would they be duties at all but for such command.

The manner in which the relation is made known, does not constitute a duty *positive*, as has been already shown in the instance of Baptism; nor does it constitute a duty *moral*, as has been also shown in the instance of religious regards to Christ.   Hence, also, we may see that positive institutions are founded either on natural religion, as Baptism in the name of the Father (though this has also a reference to the Gospel dispensation, for it is in the name of God, as the *Father of our Lord Jesus Christ*)—or on revealed religion, as Baptism in the name of the Son and of the Holy Ghost.

Secondly. From the distinction between what is moral and what is positive in religion, appears the ground of that peculiar preference which the Scripture teaches us to be due to the former.   *Positive* institutions, in *general*, as distinguished from this or that particular one, have the nature of *moral* com-

so far as they are different, we discern the reasons of the former, but not of the latter.—*Butler*.

But we are not to suppose that because we can not see the reasons for them, that God has not the wisest and best reasons for imposing them.   This would not be worth remarking, if Deistical writers, who deny the possibility of such precepts, did not confound *positive* with *arbitrary* precepts.

mands, since the reasons of them appear. Thus, for instance, the *external* worship of God is a moral duty, though no particular mode of it be so. Care, then, is to be taken, when a comparison is made between positive and moral duties, that they be compared no farther than as they are different. This being premised, should there be a moral and positive precept enjoined by the same authority, and should it be impossible, in certain conjectures, to obey both—which is to be preferred? Undoubtedly the moral. For, 1st, there is an apparent reason for the preference, and none against it, since we see the reason of the moral, but not of the positive precept. 2d. The positive institutions enjoined by Christianity are means to a moral end: and the end must be acknowledged more excellent than the means. 3d. The observance of positive institutions is no religious obedience at all, otherwise than as it proceeds from a moral principle. This is the logical way of deciding the matter; but, in a practical and more lax way of considering it, moral law and positive institutions are both alike matter of revealed command: but the Author of nature has given an intimation which is to be preferred, by writing the *moral* law upon our hearts, and interweaving it with our nature. But we are not left to reason alone; for, first, Scripture, by its general tenor and particular declarations, condemns the idea to which men have been always

prone—that peculiar positive rites constitute religion, in place of obedience to moral precepts. Secondly, in comparing positive and moral duties together, it always puts the stress of religion upon the
latter, and never upon the former; as our Lord
himself, when the Pharisees censured him for *eat-
ing with publicans and sinners*, and also when they
censured his disciples for plucking the ears of corn
on the Sabbath day, answered, "I will have mercy
and not sacrifice" (Mat., ix., 13, and xii., 7); and, by
this manner of expression, authoritatively determined, *in general*, which should have the preference: for it is as applicable to any other instance
of a comparison between positive and moral duties as to this upon which it was spoken. And
that He intended to explain wherein the *general*
spirit of religion consists, appears from the Phari-
see, on both occasions, not understanding the meaning of it; for the literal sense of the passage (Hos.,
vi.) has no difficulty in it. But as it is one of the
peculiar weaknesses of human nature, when, upon
comparison of two things, one is found to be of
greater importance than the other, to consider the
other as of scarcely any importance at all,* we

* A neglect of the *ordinances* of religion of Divine appointment is the sure system of a criminal indifference about those
higher duties by which men pretend to atone for the omission.
It is too often found to be the beginning of a licentious life,
and for the most part, ends in the highest excess of profligacy
and irreligion."—*Bishop Horsely's Sermons on the Sabbath.*

ought to remember how great presumption it is to make light of any institutions of Divine appointment, and that our obligation to obey *all* God's commands, of whatever kind they may be, are absolute and indispensable.

NOTE.—The account now given of Christianity enforces upon us the obligation of searching the Scriptures; and if there be found any passages therein, the *apparent* meaning of which is contrary to natural religion, such, we may conclude, is not the *real* meaning. But it is not at all a presumption against an interpretation of Scripture, that it contains a doctrine which the light of nature can not discover, or a precept which the law of nature does not oblige to.

L*

QUESTIONS—CHAPTER I.

1. Give summarily the scheme of the second part of this book; in which the support given to *revealed* religion by analogy is described.

2. Show the extravagance of the assertion that Revelation is in its *very notion not incredible*, as being superfluous.

3. Refute the argument that "the only design of Revelation must be to enforce the practice of *natural* piety; and it is immaterial whether we believe and practice upon the evidence of nature, or of revealed religion."

4. What are the *two views* which must be taken of Christianity, in order that we may understand its importance?

5. In what manner does the revelation of Christianity confirm and support natural religion?

6. How is it proved that this Revelation, considered only as *subservient* to natural religion, is important, as an *external* institution of it?

7. Answer the objection "that Christianity has been proved, and has had little good influence."

8. What important duties arise on our part to God the Son, and the Holy Spirit, from Christianity revealing to us the particular dispensation of Providence, carrying on through them?

9. What are the two instances by which Butler illustrates his conclusion, "that Christianity can never be esteemed of *little consequence* till it be positively supposed *false?*

10. Show clearly where is the distinction between what is *moral* and what is *positive* in religion.

11. Prove that the peculiar *preference*, which the Scripture teaches us is due to the former, is reasonable.

CHAPTER II.

OF THE SUPPOSED PRESUMPTION AGAINST A REVELATION CONSIDERED AS MIRACULOUS.

Before the positive evidence for Christianity is considered, together with the objections against that evidence, the prejudices against revelation in *general*, and the *Christian* revelation *in particular*, must be removed; to the former the present chapter is devoted.

I. There is no presumption from analogy against the general scheme of Christianity; for it is no presumption against it that it is not discoverable by reason and experience, or that it is unlike the course of nature; and there can be no other kind of presumption.

II. There is no presumption against a revelation, considered as miraculous, *in the beginning of the world*, for this is a question about a matter of *fact*, or about the extent of the exertion of an ordinary power, or about the extent of the exertion of a power called *extraordinary*, but certainly exerted.

III. There is no presumption against it from analogy *after* the settlement of a course of nature, for we have not a parallel case to compare with it, &c., &c., &c.

I. IT is commonly supposed that there is some peculiar presumption, from the analogy of nature, against the Christian scheme, at least, against miracles, so as that stronger evidence is necessary to prove the truth and reality of them than would be sufficient to convince us of other events, or matters of fact.* Now there is no appearance of a presumption, from the analogy of nature, against the

---

* Hume has gone farther; he asserts, "the credit we give to testimony is derived solely from experience"—"a miracle is *contrary* to experience."—"No testimony should ever gain credit to an event, unless it is more extraordinary that it should be false, than that the event should have happened."—"It is contrary to experience that a miracle should be true, but not contrary to experience that testimony should be false." In short, he considers miracles as *impossible*, for, speaking of the Abbé de Paris's miracles, he says, "What have we now to oppose to such a cloud of witnesses, but the *absolute impossibility* or *miraculous nature of the events they relate*." Besides the answers here given, *vide* the Introduction to "The Analogy," and that to "Paley's Evidences." The fallacy of Hume's reasoning consists in this, that he argues from the laws of matter and motion established in the world, which laws, being confessedly arbitrary constitutions of the Creator, the manner of their operation can not be drawn from any previous reasoning, but must be drawn solely from experience; but if we admit the existence of a God, we must admit that we can discover by reasoning "a priori" a connection between an Almighty cause and every effect which is the object of power. To establish his position it is necessary to prove, that nothing is possible but what is established in the usual course of nature. And as to his objection from *testimony*—for he opposes the uncertainty of testimony to the certainty of contrary experience—this is answered Infra., III. Farther, that the evidence of testimony is superior to that of experience, and that they are somewhat connected, so that the weakening of the one weakens the other, is shown in "Price's Dissertations," page 400, and in "Dr. Adam's Essay on Miracles," page 5.

general scheme of Christianity—that God created, and invisibly governs the world by Jesus Christ; and by him will hereafter judge it in righteousness; and that good men are under the secret influence of his spirit. For, if there be a presumption from analogy, it must be either because it is not discoverable by reason or experience; or else, because it is unlike the known course of nature, which is so discoverable. Now there is none on the first account, because that things lie beyond the natural reach of our faculties is no sort of presumption against the truth and reality of them; because it is certain there are innumerable things in the constitution and government of the universe which are thus beyond the natural reach of our faculties. And there is no presumption on the second account, for, in the natural government of the world, as well as in the moral government of it, we see things in a great degree unlike one another, and therefore we ought not to wonder at such unlikeness between things visible and invisible. However, the Christian and natural schemes are by no means *entirely* unlike. So that whether we call this general Christian dispensation *miraculous* or not, we see there is no presumption against it from analogy. But we are to consider miracles as visible* and invisible.

---

* A miracle is defined by Hume to be a *violation* of a law of nature, by a particular volition of the Deity, or by the interposing of an invisible agent. It is correctly defined by

The former furnish a proof of a Divine mission; the latter, being secret, do not, but require themselves to be proved by visible miracles, as, for example, the incarnation of Christ.   Revelation itself, too, is miraculous, and miracles are the proof of it —the supposed presumption against these we shall now consider.

II.   There can be no peculiar presumption from the analogy of nature against a revelation, considered as miraculous at the beginning of the world—no such presumption as is implied in the word *miraculous;* for a miracle, in its very notion, is relative to a course of nature, and implies somewhat different from it, considered as being so.   Now, either there was *no* course of nature at that time, or if there were, we do not know what the course of nature is upon the first peopling of worlds.   And therefore this is not to be considered as a question about a miracle, but as a common question of fact, admitting of the report of tradition, like other matters of fact of equal antiquity.   Or else it is a question about the *extent* to which an *ordinary* power exerted itself—a power different from the present course of nature (but not, as we have seen, to be called *miraculous*) namely, whether this power merely *made* man, or exerted itself farther *in giving him a revelation.*   Or even if the power be

others, as an extraordinary work, in which the interposition of Divine Power is clear and indisputable.

called miraculous, it will make no difference, for the power, whatever it be called, was exerted; and the question will then be, the *extent* to which an *extraordinary* power exerted itself. Against this there is as little presumption as there would be, if it were granted that our Saviour exerted miraculous powers, against his exerting it in a greater degree, or in more or fewer instances. If, then, this is a fact, admitting the testimony of tradition, what is that testimony? not that religion was reasoned out, but altogether the contrary—that it came into the world by revelation. This was mentioned in the former part of this treatise, as affording a confirmation of natural religion; and here we see it has a tendency to remove any prejudices against a *subsequent* revelation.

III. But it may be *objected* that there is some peculiar presumption from analogy against miracles; particularly against revelation, *after the settlement*, and *during the continuance of a course of nature.*

General Answer. Before we can raise an *argument* from analogy, for or against a revelation, considered as miraculous, we should be acquainted with a *similar* or *parallel* case. And nothing short of the history of a world in like circumstances with our own can be a parallel case; and had we even this, it would be but a single instance, and a presumption from it must be infinitely precarious.

PARTICULAR ANSWERS : 1st. There is a very strong presumption against common speculative truths, and against the most ordinary facts prior to the proof of them, which, yet, is overcome by almost any proof. The question, therefore, whether there be *any peculiar* presumption at all from analogy, is of no consequence; for if there be a small additional presumption against miracles, is that worth reckoning with the millions to one that there are against the most common facts ?* The only material question is, whether there be any such pre-

---

* As this has been controverted, and as it does not appear to have been Locke's opinion (for in his chapter on Probability he says, in things happening indifferently, there is nothing *for nor against* them), it may be useful to confirm the account of Butler by a passage from Price's Dissertations. " In many cases of particular histories, which are immediately believed upon the slightest testimony, there would have appeared to us, previously to this testimony, an improbability of almost infinity to one against their reality, as any one must perceive who will think how sure he is of the falsehood of all facts that have *no* evidence to support them, or which he has only *imagined* to himself. It is, then, very common for the slightest testimony to overcome an almost infinite improbability. In order to discover whether there is this improbability, let the connection of such facts with testimony be withdrawn, and then let it be considered what they are. If upon doing this, *i. e.*, upon making them objects of imagination unsupported by any proof, they became improbable, the point, I should think, will be determined; for, to find that a fact, when its connection with testimony is withdrawn, becomes improbable, is the same as to find that independently of testimony it *is* improbable.— *Vide Price's Four Dissertations.*

sumption against miracles *as to render them in any sort incredible.*

2d. Leaving out the consideration of religion, the presumption against miracles is, beyond all comparison, less than against common facts, before any evidence for either. For we are so ignorant, as to what the course of nature depends on, that there is no improbability for or against supposing that length of time may have given cause for changing it.

3d. But taking in the consideration of religion, we see distinct reasons for miracles, namely, to afford mankind instruction, additional to that of nature, and to attest the truth of it ; and this gives a positive credibility to their history in cases where these reasons hold.

4th. Miracles must not be compared to common natural events, but to the extraordinary phenomena of nature, such as comets, the power of magnetism and electricity ; and as distinguished from such phenomena there is no peculiar presumption against miracles.

M

QUESTIONS—CHAPTER II.

1. Explain what Butler means by "the general scheme of Christianity;" and show that there is no appearance of a presumption from the analogy of nature against it.

2. By what arguments does Hume attempt to prove that we ought not to believe in *any miracles?* Wherein does the fallacy of his reasoning consist?

3. Give the correct definition of a "miracle;" and illustrate by examples the *two classes*, into which they are divided, of *visible* and *invisible*.

4. Why *can* there be no *peculiar* presumption from the analogy of nature against a revelation, considered as miraculous, at the beginning of the world?

5. Describe the three views, under which *alone* the subject of a revelation *from the beginning* can be fairly considered.

6. Why may we safely admit the testimony of tradition as to the original revelation? And what is that testimony?

7. Give a general answer to the objection that "*after the settlement, and during the continuance of a course of nature*, there is a presumption from analogy against miracles."

8. What comparison does Butler draw between miracles and ordinary facts, in order to show what is the only material question respecting the former? How does Price support these assertions?

9. What weight does the consideration of *religion* add to the testimony concerning miracles?

CHAPTER III.

Objections against the scheme of Christianity, as distinguished from objections against the evidences of it are frivolous, for analogy furnishes a general answer to them.

I. That we are incompetent judges of it.

II. That it is *probable,* beforehand, that men will imagine
they have strong objections against a revelation, however
unexceptionable.

III. This leads to the determining the office of reason, namely,
to judge only of the meaning, the morality, and evidence of
revelation.

VARIOUS OBJECTIONS : The whole scheme of
Christianity is objected to ; the whole manner in
which it is put and left in the world ; several particular relations in Scripture ; things in it appearing to men *foolishness ;* things appearing matters of
offense ; the incorrectness of the style of revelation,
especially of the Prophetic parts, in consequence of
the rashness of interpreters, and the hieroglyphic

and figurative language* in which they are expressed.

I. *General Answer to all objections against Christianity considered as a matter of fact.* Upon supposition of a revelation, it is highly credible beforehand that we should be incompetent judges of it to a great degree, and that it would contain many things apparently liable to great objections in case it be judged of otherwise than by the analogy of nature. Not that the faculty of reason is to be depreciated—for it is not asserted that a supposed revelation can not be proved false from internal characters; for it may contain clear immoralities or contradictions, and either of these would prove it false; this belongs to reason to decide. (*Vide* this Chap. III.)

Proof from analogy that we are likely to be incompetent judges. If the natural and the revealed dispensations are both from God, if they coincide and together make up one scheme of Providence, our being incompetent judges of one, must render it credible that we may also be incompetent judges of the other. Since, then, upon experience, the natural dispensation is found to be greatly different from what, *before* experience, would have been expected, and is supposed to be liable to great objec-

* Thus Voltaire pretended to believe that Ezekiel eat the roll of parchment in reality, which the Prophet expressly asserts to have been a mere vision.

tions, this renders it highly credible, that if they judge of the revealed dispensation in like manner, they will find it different from expectations formed beforehand, and apparently liable to great objections. Thus, suppose a prince to govern his dominions in the wisest manner possible, by common known laws, and that upon some exigencies he should suspend them—if one of his subjects were not a competent judge beforehand of the wisdom of the *ordinary* administration, it could not be expected that he would be a competent judge of the wisdom of the *extraordinary*. Thus we see *generally* that the objections of an incompetent judgment must needs be frivolous. But let us apply these observations to a

PARTICULAR EXAMPLE. Upon supposition of a revelation, let us compare our ignorance concerning *inspiration* before experience, with our ignorance concerning *natural* knowledge. We are not judges beforehand.

1st. What degree or kind of *natural* information it were to be expected God would afford men, each by his own reason or experience; nor, 2d, how far he would enable and effectually dispose them to communicate it; nor, 3d, whether the evidence of it would be certain, highly probable, or doubtful; nor, 4th, whether it would be given with equal clearness and conviction to all; nor, 5th, whether it or the faculty of obtaining it would be given us

at once, or gradually.   In like manner, respecting
supernatural knowledge, we are ignorant beforehand, 1st, what degree of it should be expected;
2d, how far miraculous interposition would be
made to qualify men for communicating it; 3d,
whether its evidence would be certain, highly probable, or doubtful; 4th, whether its evidence would be
the same to all; and, 5th, whether the scheme should
be revealed at once or gradually—committed to writing, or left to be handed down by verbal tradition.

OBJECTION. But we *know* that a revelation, in
some of the above circumstances, one, for instance,
not committed to writing, and thus secured against
the danger of corruption, would not have answered
its purposes.

ANSWER. What purposes?   It would not have
answered all these purposes which it has now answered; but it would have answered *others*, or the
same in different degrees : and could we tell beforehand *which* were the purposes of God?   It must,
therefore, be quite frivolous to object to revelation,
in any of the fore-mentioned respects, against its being left in one way rather than another; for this
would be to object against things because they are
different from expectations, which has been shown
to be without reason.   And thus we see that the
only question concerning *the truth of Christianity*
is, whether it be a real revelation, not whether it
be attended with every circumstance which we

should have looked for ; and concerning *the authority of Scripture*, whether it be what it claims to be ; not whether it be a book of such sort, and so promulgated, as weak men imagine it should be. And therefore, neither obscurity, nor seeming inaccuracy of style, nor various readings, nor early disputes about the authors of particular parts, nor multiplied objections of this kind, could overthrow the authority of Scripture, unless the Prophets, Apostles, or our Lord had promised that it should be secure from these things. So that there are several ways of arguing, which, though just with regard to other writings, are not applicable to Scripture, at least not to the Prophetic parts of it. We can not argue that this can not be the sense of any particular passage of Scripture, for then it would have been expressed more plainly, or have been represented under a more apt figure or hieroglyphic ; yet we may justly argue thus with respect to common books, because in Scripture we are not, as we are in common books, competent judges how plainly, or under how apt an image the true sense ought to have been represented. The only question is, what appearance there is that this is the sense, and scarce any at all how much more determinately it might have been expressed.

OBJECTION. But is it not self-evident that internal improbabilities of *all kinds* weaken external probable proof?

Answer. Doubtless; but to what practical purpose can this be alleged in the present case, since internal improbabilities, which rise even to moral certainty, are overcome by the most ordinary testimony; and since we scarcely know what are improbabilities as to the matter before us.

II. The analogy of nature shows beforehand, not only that it is highly *credible men may*, but also *probable* that they *will*, imagine they have strong objections against revealed knowledge, however really unexceptionable; for so, prior to experience, they would think they had against the whole course of natural instruction. Prior to experience, they would think they had objections against the instruction which God affords to brute creatures by instincts and propensions, and to men, by these, together with reason, merely on account of the means by which such instruction is given. For instance, would it not have been thought highly improbable that men should have been so much the more capable of discovering, even to certainty, the laws of matter and of the planetary motions than the causes and cures of diseases, wherein human life appears so much more nearly concerned, or that they should discover in an instant, and unexpectedly, by the faculty of invention, what they have been in vain searching after, perhaps for years? or, that language —the only means of communicating our thoughts, should, in its very nature, be inadequate, ambiguous, and liable to abuse, both from neglect and design ? or that brutes should, in many respects, act with a sagacity and foresight often superior to what is used by man? These general observations will furnish an answer to almost all objections against Christianity, as distinguished from objections against its evidence; because these objections are no more, nor greater, than analogy shows beforehand to be highly credible that there might seem to lie against revelation. This will more clearly appear by applying these observations to a

PARTICULAR OBJECTION. The gifts said to be *miraculous*, exercised by some persons in the apostolic age in a disorderly manner, were not *really miraculous ;* for had they been so, they would have been committed to other persons, or these persons would have been endued with prudence also, or have been continually restrained in the exercise of their miraculous power.*

ANSWER. That is, in other words, God should have miraculously interposed, if at all, in a *different manner*, or *higher degree*. But from the above observations it appears undeniable, that we are not

---

* It is an objection of the same kind, and, therefore, to be answered in the same way—that the apostles were ignorant of the true nature of demoniacs ; for, even if their ignorance be admitted on this or any other point of the like kind, it can not be concluded that they could not be taught Divine truth, without a knowledge of bodily diseases, or of other points equally extraneous from the design of their mission.

judges in what degrees and manners it were to be
expected he should miraculously interpose.   Let
us look to the *natural* course of Providence, and
see are the *superior gifts* of memory, eloquence,
and knowledge conferred only on persons of prudence and decency?   And it is to be supposed that
persons endued with *miraculous* gifts, had the same
influence over them as if they were natural en-
dowments.   Farther, our natural instruction is not
always given us in a way most suited to recom-
mend it, but often with circumstances apt to prejudice us against it.

The analogy between natural and revealed instruction farther appears from this circumstance,
that the improvements and hindrances of both are
of the same kind.   *Practical*-Christianity, like the
common rules of our conduct in temporal affairs, is
plain and obvious.   The *more accurate* knowledge
of Christianity, like many parts of natural and civil
knowledge, may require exact thought and careful
consideration.   The perfect understanding of revelation, if it come to pass before the *restitution of all
things,* and without miraculous interposition, must
be arrived at in the same way as that of natural
knowledge is attained to, namely, by pursuing
hints and intimations which are generally disregarded by others.   Nor is it at all incredible that
the Bible, though so long in our possession, should
contain many truths as yet undiscovered (possibly

only to be developed by events as they come to pass); in the same way as with the same phenomena, and the same faculties of investigation, as men were possessed of long ago, great discoveries have been lately made in natural knowledge.

OBJECTION. " This analogy between natural and supernatural light fails in a material respect ; for natural knowledge is of little or no consequence."

ANSWER. We have been speaking of the *general* instruction which nature does or does not afford us. Besides, some parts of natural knowledge are of the greatest consequences. But suppose the analogy did, as it does not, fail in this respect, yet it might be abundantly supplied from the whole constitution and course of nature ; which shows that God does not dispense his gifts according to our notions of the advantages and consequence they would be to us. And this in general, with His method of dispensing knowledge in particular, would make out an analogy full to the point.

Objection against Christianity as a Remedy : " Scripture represents Christianity as an expedient to recover a lost world, to supply the deficiencies of natural light. Is it then credible that this supply should be so long withheld, and then be made known to so small a part of mankind—should be so deficient, obscure, doubtful, and liable to the like perversions and objections as the light of nature itself ?

Answer. Without determining how far this is so in fact, it is by no means incredible from analogy that it might be so; for are the remedies which nature has provided for diseases, certain, perfect, or universal?   The same principles which would lead us to conclude that they must be so, would lead us also to conclude that there could be no occasion for them, *i. e.*, that there could be no diseases at all; and these principles being found fallacious, from the fact that they are diseases, would render it credible beforehand that they may be false with respect to these remedies—as, by experience, we find they are—since the remedies of diseases are far from being certain, perfect, or universal.

III. Does it follow from all these things that reason can do nothing?   By no means, unless it follows that we are unable to judge of *any thing* from our inability to judge of *all* things.   Reason can and ought to judge (as has been partly shown already), not only of the meaning, but also of the morality and evidence of revelation.   *First*, it is the province of reason to judge of the morality of Scripture, that is, not whether it contains things different from what we should *have expected* from a wise, just, and good Being; for objections of this kind have been now obviated: but whether it contains things plainly contradictory to wisdom, justice, or goodness—to what the light of nature teaches us of God.   There is no objection of this kind against Scripture but such as would equally apply against the constitution and course of nature.

OBJECTION. But are there not some particular precepts in Scripture requiring actions immoral and vicious ?*

ANSWER. There are some requiring actions that *would be* immoral and vicious, but for such precept; but the precept changes the whole nature of the case and of the action; for these precepts are not contrary to immutable morality—they require only the doing an external action, *e. g.*, taking away the property or life of any, to which men have no right, but what arises solely from the grant of God; when this grant is revoked, they cease to have any right at all in either. If, indeed, it were required to cultivate the principles, and act from the spirit of treachery, ingratitude, cruelty, the command would not alter the nature of the case or of the action, in any of these instances. But are not these precepts liable to be perverted by designing men, and to mislead the weak and enthusiastic ? True, they are; but this is not an objection against revelation, but against the whole notion of religion as a *trial*, and against the general constitution of nature. *Secondly*, reason is to judge of the evidence of revelation, and the objections against it (which will form the subject of the

* For example, the command given by God to destroy the nation of Canaan.— *Vide Graves on the Pentateuch.*

N

7th chapter).   And it can also comprehend what is to be expected from enthusiasm and political views; and, therefore, can furnish a presumptive proof that a supposed revelation does not proceed from them, and is consequently true.

QUESTIONS—CHAPTER III.

1. Name the three principal divisions under which the subjects in this chapter are comprehended.

2. What are the various objections usually brought against the Christian revelation; and what general answer may be given to them, assuming Christianity to be a *matter of fact?*

3. Prove from *analogy* that we are likely to be *incompetent judges* as to what were to be expected in a Divine revelation.

4. State fully the particular example, in which Butler compares our ignorance concerning *inspiration, before experience,* with our ignorance concerning *natural* knowledge.

5. How is the objection obviated that " Revelation, unless given in such or such a way (*i. e.,* according to the objector's judgment of what was proper) would not *answer its purposes ?"*

6. Give the argument by which the following assertion is proved, viz., that the *analogy of nature* shows it to be probable, beforehand, that men will imagine they have strong objections against a revelation, however unexceptionable."

7. Answer the objection against Christianity, drawn from the *abuse* of gifts and powers, said to be miraculous, by persons exercising them.

8. Show that the *improvements* and *hinderances* of both natural and revealed instruction are of the *same kind.*

9. Answer the objection, that, " If Christianity be so great a remedy, why it has been so long withholden, and now so little known ?"

10. What is the proper province of *reason* in judging of revelation ?

CHAPTER IV.

OF CHRISTIANITY CONSIDERED AS A SCHEME, OR CONSTITUTION, IMPERFECTLY COMPREHENDED.

I. Admitting the credibility of Christianity as a matter of fact there may yet be objections against the wisdom, justice, and goodness of it. Analogy furnishes a *general* answer to such objections, by showing that Christianity (like God's moral government, Chap. VII., Part I.) must be a scheme beyond our comprehension.

II. This appears more clearly from particular Analogies. 1st. Means are used to accomplish ends; and, 2d, it is carried on by general laws.

III. The principal objections in *particular,* may be answered by *particular and full Analogies in Nature.* One of these objections, being against the whole scheme of Christianity, is considered here, namely. "That it supposes God to have been reduced to the necessity of using roundabout means to accomplish man's salvation."

I. IT has appeared, from the seventh chapter of the First Part, that objections against the wisdom, justice, and goodness of the constitution of nature may be answered by its being a constitution or scheme imperfectly comprehended. We now proceed to consider the like objections against revelation. And it is evident, if Christianity be a scheme, and of the same kind, the like objections against it must admit of the like answer.

Now, Christianity *is* a scheme beyond our com- prehension. The moral government and general plan of Providence is gradually proceeding, so that finally every one shall receive according to his deserts, and truth and right finally prevail. And Christianity is a particular scheme under this general plan of Providence, and a part of it conducive to its completion, consisting itself also of various parts—a mysterious economy for the recovery of the world by the Messiah (John xi., 52; and 2 Pet., iii., 13)—after successive manifestations of this great and general scheme of Providence (1 Pet., i., 11, 12)—the incarnation and passion of the Redeemer (Phil., ii.)—the miraculous mission of the Holy Ghost—the invisible government of the church— Christ's second coming to judgment, and the re-establishment of the kingdom of God (John, v., 22, 23; Mat., xxviii., 18; 1 Cor., xv.). Surely this is a scheme of things imperfectly comprehended by us; or, as the Scripture expressly asserts it to be, *a great mystery of Godliness* (1 Tim., iii., 16).

II. But this will more fully appear, by considering, 1st, that it is obvious means are made use of to accomplish ends in the Christian dispensation as much as in the natural scheme of things; and thus the things objected against, how *foolish* soever they may appear to men, may be the very best means of accomplishing the very best ends. And, 2dly, that the Christian dispensation may have been all

N*

along no less than the course of nature, carried on by general laws. To show the credibility of this, let us consider upon what grounds the *course of nature* is said to be carried on by general laws. We know several of the general laws of matter; and a great part of the natural behavior of living agents is reducible to general laws. But we know in a manner nothing by what laws storms and tempests, earthquakes, famine, pestilences become the instruments of destruction to mankind; by what laws some die as soon as they are born, and others live to extreme old age; by what laws one man is so superior to another in understanding; and innumerable other things which we know so little of as to call them *accidental*, though we know there can not be such a thing as *chance*. Thus it appears that it is from analogy—from finding that the course of nature, in *some* respects, and *so* far, goes on by general laws—that we conclude this of the rest. And if this be a just ground for such a conclusion, it is a just ground also, at least, to *render it credible*, which is sufficient for answering objections, that God's miraculous interpositions may have been all along in like manner, by *general* laws of wisdom; and, if so, there is no more reason to expect that every exigence should be provided for by them than that every exigence in nature should be by the general laws of nature.

III. *Objected against the whole scheme of Christ-*

ianity: "The Gospel scheme seems to suppose, that God was reduced to the necessity of a long series of intricate means in order to accomplish His ends—the recovery and salvation of the world; just as men, for want of understanding or power, are forced to go roundabout ways to arrive at their ends."

ANSWER. The use of means is the system of nature (and means which we often think tedious). The change of seasons, the ripening of the fruits of the earth, the very history of a flower is an instance of this. Rational creatures form their characters by the gradual accession of knowledge; our existence, too, is successive, and one state of life is appointed to be a preparation for another. Men are impatient, and for precipitating things—the Author of nature appears deliberate throughout His operations. This is a plain answer to the objection; but we are greatly ignorant how far things are considered, by the Author of nature, under the single notion of means and ends, so as that it may be said, this is merely an end, and that merely means, in His regard.

QUESTIONS—CHAPTER IV.

1. In obviating objections against the wisdom, justice, and goodness of Christianity, with what does Butler compare it; and what connection does he assert to exist between it and the general *plan* of Providence?

2. Name two particular analogies, by the consideration of which the credibility of Christianity being a scheme imperfectly comprehended by us, will more fully appear.

3. Upon what grounds is it said that the *course of nature* is carried on by *general laws?* What inference may be drawn from this subject, applicable to miraculous interpositions?

4. How may the principal objections in *particular* against Christianity be answered?

5. Answer the following particular objection, viz., "The Gospel scheme supposes God to have been reduced to the necessity of using roundabout means to accomplish man's salvation."

CHAPTER V.

OF THE PARTICULAR SYSTEM OF CHRISTIANITY—THE
APPOINTMENT OF A MEDIATOR, AND THE REDEMP-
TION OF THE WORLD BY HIM.

I. Proceeding to answer other Particular Objections.—Analogy shows that there can be no objection against the *general notion of a Mediator.*

II. This analogy appears more fully upon the supposition of
future punishments following in the way of natural consequences.

III. The Analogy of Nature shows that there is no probability
that behaving well for the future, or any thing that *we*
could do, would alone, and of itself, prevent the consequences of vice.

IV. The Scripture view of Redemption explained, and two
Objections against the Atonement answered, viz., "That we
can not see the efficacy of it, and that it represents the innocent as suffering for the guilty."

I. THE whole analogy of nature removes all imagined presumption against the *general* notion of a
Mediator between God and man; for we find all
living creatures are brought into the world, and
their life, in infancy, is preserved by the instrumen-

tality of others ; and every satisfaction of it is bestowed by the like means. Is not then the supposition that His *invisible* government is, in part, at
least, carried on by the like means as credible as
the contrary ? The light of nature, therefore, furnishes no presumption against the *general* notion of
a mediator* (and it is against this that the objection
is urged, not against mediation in that high, eminent, and peculiar sense in which Christ is our
Mediator), since we find by experience that God
does appoint mediators to be the instruments of
good and evil to us—the instruments of His justice
and His mercy.

II. The moral government of the world (which
must be supposed before we can consider the revealed doctrine of its redemption by Christ) implies
that the consequence of vice shall be misery in
some future state, by the righteous judgment of
God ; but since we are altogether unacquainted

* The instances of Codrus, the last Athenian king, exposing
himself to *inevitable* death; and Marcus Curtius, a noble
Roman, leaping into the gulf, have been both considered,
from the certainty of the offering, and the feelings of their
respective nations, as proofs of a disposition in mankind to
think that the voluntary and certain death of a person reputed
noble and innocent (Pliny says of Curtius, " *virtute ac pietate
ac morte præclara expleverat*"), may prevent impending and
Divinely threatened calamities. *Vide* the Epistle to the Romans, v., 7, 8. " For scarcely for a *righteous* man will one
die; yet peradventure for a *good* man some would even dare
to die. But God commendeth his love towards us, in that
while we were yet *sinners* Christ died for us."

how future punishment is to follow wickedness, there is no absurdity in supposing that it may follow of course, or in the way of natural consequence, from God's original constitution of the world (in the same way as many miseries follow particular courses of action at present)—from the nature He has given us, and from the condition in which He places us; or in like manner, as a person rashly trifling upon a precipice falls down, breaks his limbs, and without help perishes—all in the way of natural consequence.

OBJECTION. Is not this taking the execution of justice out of the hands of *God*, and giving it to *nature?*

ANSWER. When things come to pass according to the course of nature, this does not prevent them from being His doing, who is the God of nature; and Scripture ascribes those punishments to Divine justice, which are known to be *natural*. Yet, after all, this supposition is of no consequence, but a mere illustration of our argument; for, as it must be admitted that future punishment is not a matter of arbitrary appointment, but of reason, equity, and justice, so it amounts to perhaps the same thing, whether they follow by a natural consequence or in any other way. *Without* this supposition, we have a sufficient analogy, but with it, we have a *full* analogy in the course of nature for a provision made for preventing the future consequences of

vice from following inevitably, and in all cases.
For there is at present a provision made, that all
the *bad natural consequences* of men's actions should
not always actually follow, but should in certain
degrees be prevented.   As the Author of nature
permits evil, so He has provided reliefs, and in
many cases, perfect remedies for it—reliefs and
remedies even for that evil which is the fruit of our
own misconduct, and which otherwise would have
ended in our destruction.   And this is an instance
both of severity and of indulgence in the constitution of nature.   Thus *all* the bad consequences,
now mentioned, of a man's trifling upon a precipice
might be prevented ; or *some*, at least, by the assistance of others, in obedience to the suggestion of
their nature, and by this assistance being accepted.
Now, suppose the constitution of nature were otherwise; that the natural bad consequences of actions,
foreseen to have such consequences, could not, *in
any instance*, be prevented, after the actions were
committed, no one can say whether such a more
severe constitution of things might not have been
really good.   But the contrary being the case, this
may be called mercy or compassion, in the original
constitution of the world—*compassion*, as distinguished from *goodness in general*.   Therefore, the
whole known constitution and course of things affording us instances of such compassion, it would
be according to the analogy of nature to hope that

however ruinous the natural consequences of vice might be, from the general laws of God's government over the universe; yet provision might be made, possibly might have been *originally* made, for preventing these ruinous consequences from inevitably following, at least from following universally and in all cases. Some will, perhaps, wonder at finding it spoken of as at all *doubtful*, that the ruinous consequences of vice might be prevented, having scarcely any apprehension or thought at all concerning the matter. But, judging from the present scene, we find the effects of even rashness and neglect are often extreme misery, irretrievable ruin, and even death. Now, it is natural to apprehend that the bad consequences of irregularity will be greater in proportion as the irregularity is so. And there is no comparison between these irregularities and the greater instances of vice, whereby mankind have presumptuously introduced confusion and misery into the kingdom of God. So that, as no one can say in what degree fatal the unprevented consequences of vice may be, according to the general rule of Divine government, so it is, by no means, intuitively certain, how far these consequences could possibly be prevented, consistently with the eternal rule of right, or with what is, in fact, the moral constitution of nature. However, there would be large ground to hope, that the universal government was not so severely strict, but

O

that there was room for pardon, or for having these penal consequences prevented. Yet,

III. There seems no probability that any thing we could do would alone, and of itself, prevent them; for we do not know all the reasons which render future punishments necessary, nor all the natural consequences of vice, nor in what manner they would follow if unprevented, and, therefore, we can not say whether we could do any thing which would be sufficient to prevent them. Farther, that repentance and reformation alone, and by itself, is wholly insufficient to prevent the future consequences of vice,* or to put us in the condition in which we should have been had we preserved our innocence, appears plainly credible from analogy; for we see it does not avail in a much lower capacity. In their temporal capacity, men ruin their fortunes, and bring on diseases, by extravagance and excess. Will sorrow for these follies

---

* The case of *penitence* is clearly different from that of *innocence*—it implies a mixture of guilt precontracted, and punishment proportionably deserved; it is consequently inconsistent with *rectitude* that both should be treated alike by God. The present conduct of the penitent will receive God's approbation; but the reformation of the sinner can not have a retrospective effect; the agent may be changed, but his former sins can not be thereby canceled. The convert and the sinner are the same individual person, and the agent must be answerable for his whole conduct.—*Balguy's Essay on Redemption.*

Cicero goes no farther on this head than to assert—Quem pœnitet peccasse, *pene* est innocens.—*Dr. Shuckford.*

past, and behaving well for the future, alone and of itself, prevent the natural consequences of them? On the contrary, their natural abilities of helping themselves are often impaired; or, if not, yet they are absolutely forced to seek assistance from others for retrieving their affairs.

2d. It is contrary to all our notions of government, that reformation alone would prevent *all* the judicial bad consequences of having done evil :* and though it might prevent them in some cases, yet we could not determine in what degree and in what cases it would do so.

3d. It is also contrary to the general sense of mankind, as appears from the general prevalence of propitiatory sacrifices over the heathen world.†

IV. In this darkness, or this light of nature, call

---

* If it be said that this would not be proper in human governments, because they may easily be deceived by false shows of repentance; I answer, that, supposing human governors could certainly distinguish a true repentance from a false one, the inconvenience of such a constitution to the public would still be the same; for it would encourage persons to commit crimes, in hopes of doing it with impunity, since every criminal would think that, in order to escape punishment, he had nothing more to do but to repent, and that this alone would satisfy the law; and he would be apt to flatter himself that this was at any time in his power.—*Leland against Tindal.*

† That the heathen supposed their animal sacrifices to be not only of an *expiatory*, but of a *vicarious* nature, might be shown from a variety of passages. The following from the Book of Ovid's Fasti is full to the point :

"Cor pro corde, precor, pro fibris, sumite fibras
Hanc animam vobis pro meliore damus."

it which you please, Revelation comes in—confirms every doubting fear which could enter into the heart of man concerning the future unprevented consequence of wickedness—supposes the world to be in a state of ruin (a supposition which seems the very groundwork of the Christian dispensation, and which, if not provable by reason, yet is in no wise contrary to it)—teaches us too, that the rules of Divine government are such as not to admit of pardon immediately and directly upon repentance, or by the sole efficacy of it; but then teaches, at the same time, what nature might justly have hoped, that the moral government of the universe was not so rigid but that there was room for an interposition; and that God hath mercifully provided this interposition to prevent the destruction of the human kind. *"God so loved the world, that he gave his only begotten Son, that whosoever believeth in him* (*i. e.*, in a practical sense) *should not perish."* He gave his Son in the same way of goodness to the world as He affords particular persons the friendly assistance of their fellow-creatures; when without it, their temporal ruin would be the certain consequence of their follies—in the same *way* of goodness, I say, though in a transcendent and infinitely higher *degree.* And the Son of God *loved us, and gave himself for us*, with a love which he himself compares to that of human friendship; though, in this case, all comparisons must fall infinitely short of the thing intended to be illustrated by them. He interposed in such a manner as to prevent the *appointed* or *natural* punishment that would otherwise have been executed upon them.* Nor is there any thing here inconsistent with Divine goodness; for were we to suppose the constitution of things to be such that the whole creation must have perished, but for something appointed by God to prevent it, even this supposition would not be inconsistent, in any degree, with the most absolutely perfect goodness.

* It can not, I suppose, be imagined, that it is affirmed or implied, in any thing said in this chapter, that none can have the benefit of the general redemption but such as have the advantage of being made acquainted with it in the present life. But it may be needful to mention, that several questions, which have been brought into the subject before us, and determined, are not in the least entered into here—questions which have been, I fear, rashly determined, and, perhaps, with equal rashness contrary ways. For instance, "Whether God could have saved the world by other means than the death of Christ; consistently with the general laws of his government?" And "Had not Christ come into the world, what would have been the future condition of the better sort of men—those just persons over the face of the earth, for whom Manasses, in his prayer, asserts repentance was not appointed?" The meaning of the first of these questions is greatly ambiguous; and neither of them can properly be answered without going upon that infinitely absurd supposition that we know the whole of the case. And, perhaps, the very inquiry, *What would have followed, if God had not done as he has?* may have in it some very great impropriety, and ought not to be carried on any farther than is necessary to help our partial conceptions of things.—*Butler.*

o*

OBJECTION. But Christianity supposes mankind to be naturally in a very strange state of degradation.

ANSWER. This is true, but it is not Christianity which has put us into this state, and there will be little reason to object against the Scripture account, if we consider the miseries and wickedness of the world ; the wrongness which the best experience within themselves ; and that the natural appearances of human degradation were so strong, that the heathen moralists inferred it from them, and that the earth, our habitation, has the appearances of being a ruin.   It was, according to Scripture, the crime of our first parents that placed us in this state, and this account of the occasion of our being placed in a more disadvantageous condition is particularly analogous to what we see in the daily course of natural Providence, as the recovery of the world by Christ has been shown to be so in general.

But let us consider the Scripture account of the particular manner in which Christ interposed in the redemption of the world, or his office of mediator, in the largest sense between God and man. *He is the light of the world**—the revealer of the will of God in the most eminent sense.   He is a propitiatory sacrifice†—*the Lamb of God‡*—our High

* John, i., and viii., 12.

† Rom., iii., 25, and v., 11 ; Cor., v., 7 ; Eph., v., 2 ; 1 John, ii., 2 ; Mat., xxvi., 28.

‡ John, i., 29, 36, and throughout the Book of Revelation.

CHAP. V.]   SYSTEM OF CHRISTIANITY.   163

Priest*—and, what seems of peculiar weight, he is
described beforehand, in the Old Testament, under
the same characters of a Priest and an expiatory
victim.†

OBJECTION. Christ's atonement is merely by way
of allusion to the sacrifices of the Mosaic law.

ANSWER. The Apostle, on the contrary, asserts,
that the "law was a shadow of good things to
come;"‡ that the Levitical priesthood was a shadow
or type of the priesthood of Christ (Heb., viii., 4,
5), in like manner, as the tabernacle made by Moses, was a copy of that shown him in the mount.
Nor can any thing be more express than the following passage: "It is not possible that the blood
of bulls and of goats should take away sin. Where-
fore, when he cometh into the world, he saith, sacrifice and offering (i. e., of bulls and goats) thou
wouldest not, but a body hast thou prepared me.
Lo! I come to do thy will, O God.   By the which
will we are sanctified through the offering of the
body of Jesus Christ once for all."   Heb., x., 4, 5,
7, 9, 10.   Again, " Christ was once offered to bear
the sins of many, and unto them that look for him
shall he appear the second time, without sin, unto
salvation."   Heb., ix., 28.   Without sin, i. e., without bearing sin—without being a sin-offering.

* Throughout the Epistle to the Hebrews.
† Is., liii.; Dan., ix., 24; Ps., cx., 4.
‡ Heb., x., 1.

Moreover, Scripture declares that there is an efficacy in what Christ did and suffered for us, additional to and beyond mere instruction, example, and government. That Jesus should die for that nation (the Jews), and not for that nation only, *but that also*, plainly by the efficacy of his death, he should gather together in one the children that are scattered abroad ;* that he suffered for sins, the just for the unjust ;† *that he gave his life—himself a ransom ;‡ that he is our advocate, intercessor, and propitiation.*

Let us now consider the nature of Christ's office, according to the three heads under which it is usually treated of, namely Prophet, Priest, and King, reserving the second head for the last, in order to answer the objections against it. *First.* He was, by way of eminence, the Prophet—*that Prophet that should come into the world*§ to declare the Divine will. He taught authoritatively ; He gave to the moral system of nature the additional evidence of testimony ; He distinctly revealed the manner in which God would be worshipped, the efficacy of

---

* John, xi., 51, 52.   † 1 Pet., iii., 18.

‡ Mat., xx., 29. *Vide*, also, Mark, x., 45 ; 1 Tim., ii., 6 ; 2 Pet., ii., 1 ; Rev., xiv., 4 ; 1 Cor., vi., 20 ; 1 Pet., i., 19 ; Rev., v., 9 ; Gal., iii., 13 ; Heb., vii., 25 ; 1 John, ii., 1, 2 ; Heb., ii., 10, and v., 9 ; 2 Cor., v., 19 ; Rom., v., 10 ; Eph., ii., 16 ; Heb., ii., 14. See also a remarkable passage in the Book of Job, xxxiii., 24 ; Phil., ii., 8, 9 ; John, iii., 35, and v., 22, 23 ; Rev., v., 12, 13.

§ John, vi., 14.

repentance, and a future state of rewards and punishments; and He set us a perfect *example, that we should follow his steps. Secondly.* He is a King, as he has a kingdom which is not of this world. He founded a visible church, to be a standing memorial of religion, and invitation to it; over this He exercises an invisible government, "for the perfecting of the saints—for the edifying his body."* All persons who live in obedience to his laws are members of this church, and for these *he is gone to prepare a place, and will come again to receive them to himself;*† and likewise to *take vengeance on those that know not God, and obey not his Gospel.*‡

Against these parts of Christ's office there are no objections, but what are fully obviated in the beginning of this chapter.

Thirdly. As to the priesthood of Christ, he offered himself a propitiatory sacrifice for the sins of the world. Expiatory sacrifices were commanded the Jews, and obtained among other nations from traditions, the original of which was probably revelation. These were continually repeated. "But now, once in the end of the world, Christ appeared to put away sin, by the sacrifice of himself."§ How the atonement has this efficacy, which the heathen sacrifices had not, and the Jewish had only in a

---

* Eph., iv., 12.   † John, xiv., 2; Rev., iii., 21, and xi., 15.
‡ 2 Thes., i., 8.   § Heb., ix., 26.

very limited degree, Scripture has not revealed to
us.   Some have gone beyond what the Scripture
has authorized in explaining it; and others, because they could not explain it, have rejected it,
and confine the office of Christ, as Redeemer of the
world, to his instruction, example, and government
of the church.   Whereas the Gospel doctrine is,
not only that He taught the efficacy of repentance,
but that He made it of the efficacy which it is, by
what He did and suffered for us; that he revealed
to sinners that they were in a capacity of salvation,
and how they might obtain it, and also put them
in that capacity.

1st OBJECTION. We do not see the necessity or
expediency of the sacrifice of Christ.

ANSWER. Our ignorance with regard to the
means, manner, and occasion of future punishments, and with regard to the nature of future
happiness, shows evidently that we are not judges,
antecedently to revelation, whether a Mediator was
or was not necessary.   And for the very same
reasons, *upon supposition of the necessity of a Mediator*, we are not judges, antecedently to revelation,
of the whole nature of his office.   And, therefore,
no objection can be urged against any part of that
office, until it can be shown positively not to be
requisite to the ends proposed, or that it is in itself
unreasonable.   There seems to be something of
this positive kind in this.

2d Objection. " The doctrine of Christ's being appointed to suffer for the sins of the world, represents God as being indifferent whether he punished the innocent or the guilty."

Answer. 1. This is not an objection against Christianity merely ; but concludes as much against the constitution of nature, since, in the daily course of natural providence, it is appointed that innocent persons should suffer for the guilty.   The objection does not apply the more against the appointment in Christianity, because it is of infinitely greater importance, since notwithstanding, it may be, as it plainly is, an appointment of the *same kind*, but it would apply (if it had any force) more against the appointment in nature, where we are commanded, and even necessitated, to suffer for the faults of others ; whereas the sufferings of Christ were *voluntary*.   Yet, there is no objection to the former ; for, upon the completion of the moral scheme every one shall receive according to his deserts.   But during the progress of this scheme, vicarious punishments may be fit and absolutely necessary.   2d. This method of our redemption is unanswerably justified by its apparent natural tendency—its tendency to vindicate the authority of God's laws, and to deter his creatures from sin.

This (though by no means an account of the whole of the case) would be a sufficient answer to objections of the foregoing kind, which are insisted

upon, either from ignorance of what are to be considered God's appointments, or forgetfulness of the
daily instances of this case in those appointments;
and, from this ignorance or forgetfulness, together
with their inability of seeing how the sufferings of
Christ could contribute to the redemption of the
world, unless by arbitrary and tyrannical will, they
conclude that they could not contribute to it any
other way.   But to see the absurdity of such an
objection against Christianity, or, as it really is,
against the constitution of nature, let us consider
what it amounts to—that a Divine appointment can
not be necessary or expedient, because the object-
or does not discern it to be so, though he must
own that the nature of the case is such as renders
him incapable of judging whether it be so or not,
or of seeing it to be necessary, though it were so!
The presumption of this kind of objections to particular things revealed in Scripture, seems almost
lost in the folly of them; and the folly of them is
yet greater, when they are urged, as usually they
are, against things in Christianity analogous or like
to those natural dispensations of Providence which
are matter of experience.   And the absurdity is
still farther heightened by the consideration that
we are not actively concerned in the parts, the expediency of which can not be understood, for these
relate to the Divine conduct, which is a very different subject from *our duty*, with respect to which

none need plead want of information.   The constitution of the world, and God's natural government over it, is all a mystery, as much as the Christian dispensation.   Yet, under the first, He has given men all things pertaining to life (though it is but an infinitely small part of natural providence which experience teaches us), and, under the others, all things pertaining unto godliness. There is no obscurity in the common precepts of Christianity ; though, if there were, a Divine command ought to impose the strongest obligation to obedience.   But the reasons of all the Christian precepts are evident.   Positive institutions are necessary to keep up and propagate religion.   The internal and external worship which we owe to Christ arises out of what He has done and suffered for us—out of His authority, and the relation He (according to revelation) stands in to us.

P

QUESTIONS—CHAPTER V.

1. Show that there can be no objection from analogy against the *general notion* of a Mediator.

2. In reasoning upon the redemption of the world, what *supposition* may we, without absurdity, assume, respecting the way in which punishment may follow sin ?

3. Answer the objection that "supposing punishment to be the *natural consequence* of sin, is taking the execution of justice out of the hands of God."

4. Give fully the argument illustrating the assertion that "with this supposition, we have a full analogy, in the course of nature, for a provision made for preventing the future consequences of vice from following inevitably and in all cases."

5. How may we prove the unreasonableness of those who wonder at finding it spoken of as at all *doubtful* that the ruinous consequences of vice might have been prevented ?

6. What considerations show the improbability that behaving well for the future, or any thing that we could do, would alone, and of itself, prevent the fatal consequences of vice ?

7. What confirmation is given to the teaching of the light of nature by the Scriptural view of man's redemption ?

8. Prove that there is no weight in the objection that " Christianity supposes mankind to be naturally in a very *strange* state of degradation."

9. Explain at large, under three different heads, the *particular manner* in which Christ interposed in the redemption of the world.

10. Against what part of Christ's office have most objections been urged, and how have men erred on contrary sides in their reasonings concerning it ?

11. Answer the following objections : 1st. We do not see the necessity or expediency of the sacrifice of Christ.

12. 2d Objection. The doctrine of Christ's being appointed to suffer for the sins of the world, represents God as being indifferent whether He punished the innocent or the guilty.

13. By what arguments does Butler expose the presumption and folly of these, and similar objections, to particular things revealed in Scripture ?

CHAPTER VI.

OF THE WANT OF UNIVERSALITY IN REVELATION,
AND OF THE SUPPOSED DEFICIENCY IN THE PROOF
OF IT.

I. The next Objections to be considered are, 1. That Revelation is left upon doubtful evidence, and, therefore, it can not be true. 2. Revelation is not Universal, and, therefore, can not be true. These Objections are answered by full Analogies in the Constitution of Nature.

II. Admitting Revelation to be uncertain in its evidence, the three following practical reflections will tend to remove all causes of complaint: 1. The evidence of Religion not appearing obvious, may constitute one particular part of some men's *Trial*, in the religious sense. 2. Doubting implies some degree of evidence, and puts men into a *general state of Probation*, in the moral and religious sense; and consequently, 3. These difficulties are no more to be complained of than *external* circumstances of temptation.

III. But this uncertainty may partly arise from our own neglect.

IV. An apparent Analogy against the fitness of doubtful evidence answered.

I. IT has been objected, 1st, that if the evidence of revelation appears doubtful, this itself turns into a positive argument against it; because it can not be supposed that, if it were really true, it would be left to subsist upon doubtful evidence; 2d, that revelation can not be true from its want of Universality.

Now the weakness of these objections may be shown by observing the suppositions upon which they are founded, which are really such as these : 1. It can not be thought that God would bestow any favor at all upon us unless in the degree we imagine might be most to our particular advantage ; and, 2, that it can not be thought he would bestow a favor upon any, unless he bestowed the same upon all.

General Answer to the 1st Objection. Let the objectors to revelation, on account of its supposed doubtfulness, consider what that evidence is which they act upon with regard to their *temporal* interests. There are various circumstances which render it uncertain and doubtful ; such as the difficulty and almost impossibility of balancing pleasure and pain, to see on which side the overplus lies— of making allowances for the difference of feeling which we may have, when we have obtained the object in view—and of the casualties which may prevent our obtaining it, *e. g.*, sudden death— the danger of our being deceived by the appearances of things, especially if we are inclined to favor deceit. Yet all this is considered to be justly disregarded, upon account of there appearing

P*

greater advantages in case of success, though there be but little probability of it ; and even when the probability is greatly against success, if there be only a *possibility* that we may succeed.

General Answer to the 2d Objection. These objectors should observe that the Author of nature, in numberless instances, bestows upon some what he does not upon others who seem equally in need of it ; for instance, health and strength, capacities of prudence and of knowledge, riches, and all external advantages ; and, notwithstanding these varieties and uncertainties, God exercises a natural government over the world ; and there is such a thing as a prudent and imprudent institution of life, with regard to our health and our affairs under this government.

Now, let us more particularly consider what is to be found in the evidence and reception of revelation analogous to the preceding, and we will see farther the futility of these objections. As neither the Jewish nor Christian revelation has been universal, and, as they have been afforded to a greater or less part of the world at different times, so likewise at different times, both revelations have had different degrees of evidence. The Jews who lived during the succession of prophets, that is, from Moses till after the captivity, had higher evidence of the truth of their religion than those had who lived in the interval between the captivity and the coming of Christ. And the first Christians had higher evidence of the miracles wrought in attestation of Christianity than we have now. They had also a strong presumptive proof of the truth of it, of which we have little remaining—the presumptive proof from the influence which it had upon the lives of the generality of its professors. And we, or future ages, may possibly have a proof of it, which they could not have, from the conformity between the prophetic history, and the state of the world and of Christianity. And, farther, if we were to suppose the evidence which some have of religion to amount to little more than seeing that it *may* be true; others to have a *full conviction* of its truth; and others severally to have all the intermediate degrees of evidence between these two; if we put the case that revelation, for the present, was only intended to be a small light in the midst of a world greatly overspread with darkness, so that some at a remote distance might receive some glimmerings of it, and yet not be able to discern its origin; and others, in a nearer situation, should have its light obscured in different ways and degrees; and others within its clearer influence, enlivened and directed by it, and yet, even to these, that it should be no more than *a light shining in a dark place;* all this would be perfectly uniform with the conduct of Providence in the distribution of His other blessings. If the fact of the case really

were, that *some* have received no light at all from
Scripture, as many heathen nations; that *others*
have had, by this means, natural religion enforced
upon them, but never had Scripture revelation,
with its real evidence, proposed to them, like, perhaps, the ancient Persians and modern Moham-
medans; that *others* have had revelation proposed
to them, but with such interpolations in its system,
and with its evidence so blended with false miracles, &c., as to produce doubt and uncertainty, which
may be the case with some thoughtful men in most
Christian nations; and, lastly, that *others* have Christianity proposed to them in its proper light, but
yet not light sufficient to satisfy curiosity. Now,
if this be a true account of the degrees of moral
and religious light and evidence, there is nothing
in it but may be paralleled by manifest analogies in
the present natural dispensations of Providence.

But does not this unequal distribution appear
harsh and unjust? By no means; for every one
shall be equitably dealt with: no more shall be
required of any one than what might have been
equitably expected of him, from the circumstances
in which he was placed: *i. e.*, every man *shall be
accepted according to what he had, not according to
what he had not.* This, however, doth not imply
that all persons' condition here is equally advantageous with respect to futurity; and their being
placed in darkness is no more a reason why per-

sons should not endeavor to get out of it, and why others should not endeavor to bring them out of it, than it is a reason why ignorant people should not endeavor to learn, or should not be instructed.

II. What, in general, may be the account or reason of these things ?   It is not unreasonable to suppose that the same wise and good principle, whatever it was, which disposed the Author of nature to make *different* kinds and orders of creatures, disposed Him also to place creatures of the *like* kinds in *different* situations : and that the same principle which disposed Him to make creatures of *different moral* capacities, disposed Him to place creatures of *like moral* capacities, in *different religious* situations, and even the *same* creatures, at *different* periods of their being.   And the account, or reason of this, is also, most probably, the account why the constitution of things is such, that creatures of moral capacities, for a considerable part of their life, are not all subjects of morality and religion.

But can we not give a more *particular* account of these things ?   Here we must be greatly in the dark,* were it only that we know so very little, even

---

* To expect a distinct, comprehensive view of the whole subject, clear of difficulties and objections, is to forget our nature and condition, neither of which admit of such knowledge with respect to any science whatever : and to inquire with this expectation, is not to inquire as a man, but as one of another order of creatures.—*Butler's Sermon on the Ignorance of Man.*

of our own case. We are in the midst of a system; our present state probably connected with the past, as it is with the future. A *system* in its very notion implies variety, so that *were revelation universal*, yet from men's different capacities of understanding, from the different lengths of their lives, from their difference of education, temper, and bodily constitution, their religious situations would be widely different, and the disadvantages of some in comparison to others would be altogether as much as at present; and the true account of our being placed here must be supposed also to be the true account of our ignorance of the reasons of it. But the following *practical reflections* may deserve the consideration of those persons who think the circumstances of mankind, or their own, in the fore-mentioned respects, a subject of complaint. 1st. The evidence of religion not appearing obvious, may constitute one particular part of some men's trial, in the religious sense, as it gives scope for a virtuous exercise, or vicious neglect of their understanding, in examining, or not examining, into that evidence. There seems no possible reason to be given why we may not be in a state of moral probation with regard to the exercise of our understanding upon the subject of religion, as we are with regard to our behavior in common affairs. For religion is not intuitively true, but a matter of deduction and inference; a conviction of its truth is not forced upon every one, but left to be by some collected by heedful attention to premises. The careful and solicitous examination of the evidence of religion *before* conviction, is an exercise of the same inward principle that renders a person obedient to its precepts *after* conviction; and neglect is as much real depravity in the one case as in the other.

2d. Even if the evidence of religion were, in the highest degree, doubtful, it would put men into a *general state of probation*, in the moral and religious sense. For, suppose a man to be really in doubt whether such a person had not done him the greatest favor, or whether his whole temporal interest was not depending on that person, he could not consider himself (if he had any sense of gratitude or of prudence) in the same situation as if he had no such doubt; or as if he were certain he had received no favor from such a person, or that he no way depended upon him. So that, considering the infinite importance of religion, there is not so great a difference as is generally imagined between what ought in reason to be the rule of life to those who really doubt and those who are fully convinced of the truth of religion.* Their hopes, and fears, and

* For would it not be madness for a man to forsake a safe road, and prefer to it one in which he acknowledges there is an even chance he should lose his life, though there were an even chance, likewise, of his going safe through it? Yet there are people absurd enough to take the supposed doubtfulness of religion for the same thing as a proof of its falsehood,

obligations will be in various degrees; but as the subject-matter of their hopes and fears is the same, so the subject-matter of their obligations is not so very unlike.   For doubting gives occasion and motives to consider farther the important subject; to preserve a sense that they may be under the Divine moral government, and an awful solicitude about religion, so as to bind them to refrain from all immorality and profaneness; and such conduct will tend to improve in them that character which the practice of religion would in those fully convinced of its truth.   And they are farther accountable for their *example*, if with a character for understanding, or in a situation of influence in the world, they disregard all religion, though doubtful to them; and *very accountable*, as they may do more injury this way, or might do more good by the opposite, than by acting ill or well, in the common intercourse among mankind.

The ground of these observations is, that doubting necessarily implies some degree of evidence for that of which we doubt: for no person would be in doubt concerning the truth of a number of facts, accidentally entering his mind, and of which he had

after they have concluded it doubtful, from hearing it often called in question.   This shows how infinitely unreasonable skeptical men are with regard to religion, and that they really lay aside their reason, upon this subject, as much as the most *extravagant enthusiast.—Butler's Charge.*

no evidence at all.   In the case of an even chance, we should commonly say we had no evidence at all for either side ; yet this case is equivalent to all others, where there is such evidence on both sides of a question as leaves the mind in doubt concerning the truth : and in all these cases, although there is no more evidence on the one side than on the other, there is much more for either than for the truth of a number of random thoughts.   And thus, it will appear that there are as many degrees between no evidence at all, and that degree of it which affords ground for doubt, as there are between that degree which is the ground of doubt, and demonstration.   And it is as real an imperfection in the *moral character*, not to be influenced by a lower degree of evidence, when discerned, as it is in the *understanding* not to discern it.   The lower degrees of evidence will be discerned or overlooked, according to the fairness and honesty of men, as in speculative matters, according to their capacity of understanding.

3dly. The speculative difficulties in which the evidence of religion is involved, are no more a just ground of complaint than external circumstances of temptation, or than difficulties in the practice of it, after a full conviction of its truth.   (And there is no ground for objection here, for temptations render our state a more improving state of discipline, by giving occasion to a more attentive and continued exercise

Q

of the virtuous principle.) Now, it will appear, that the same account may be given of the doubtful evidence of religion, as of temptation and difficulties, with regard to practice; for they belong to a state of probation. (1st.) As implying *trial* and *difficulties*. The doubtfulness of its evidence affords opportunities to an unfair mind of explaining away and deceitfully hiding from itself that evidence which it might see, and of being flattered with the hopes of escaping the consequences of vice; though it is clearly seen that these hopes are, at least, uncertain, in the same way as the common temptation to many instances of folly, which end in temporal infamy and ruin, is the ground for hope of not being detected, and of escaping with impunity, *i. e.*, *the doubtfulness of the proof beforehand* that such foolish behavior will thus end in infamy and ruin. The examination of this evidence requires an attentive, solicitous, and, perhaps, *painful* exercise of the understanding. And there are circumstances in men's situations, in their temporal capacities, analogous to those concerning religion. In *some* situations the chief difficulty, with regard to conduct, is not the doing what is prudent when it is known, but the principal exercise is recollection, and being guarded against deceit. In *other* situations, the principal exercise is attention, in order to discover what is the prudent part to act.

(2d.) This, and, indeed, temptation in general, as

it calls forth some virtuous efforts additional to
what would otherwise have been wanting, can not
but be an *additional discipline and improvement of
virtue*, nay, may form the *principal* part of some
persons' trial; for as the chief temptations of the
generality of the world are the ordinary motives to
injustice or pleasure, or to live in the neglect of
religion, from a frame of mind almost insensible to
any thing distant, so there are others, without this
shallowness of temper, of a deeper sense as to what
is invisible and future, who, from their natural constitution and external condition, may have small
temptations and difficulties in the common course
of life.   Now, when these latter persons have a
full conviction of the truth of religion, its practice is
to them almost unavoidable; yet these persons may
need discipline and exercise in a higher degree
than they would have by such an easy practice of
religion.

(3d.) This may be necessary for their probation
in the third sense of the word,* for a farther manifestation of their moral character to the creation of
God, than such a practice of it would be.

III. But all the preceding reflections suppose
that men's dissatisfaction with the evidence of religion, does not arise from their neglect or prejudices; but may it not be owing to their own fault?
Levity, carelessness, passion, and *prejudice do* hin-

* *Vide* Chap. IV., Part I.

der us from being rightly informed with respect to common things, and they *may* in like manner (and perhaps in some farther providential manner) hinder us with respect to moral and religious subjects. But does not the Scripture declare that every one *shall not understand?*[*]   Certainly.   But it does not determine how this shall be effected; and it makes no difference whether it be effected by the evidence of Christianity being originally and with design so ordered, as that those who are desirous of evading moral obligations should not see it, and that honest-minded persons should;[†] or whether it come to pass by any other means.   Farther, the general proof of *natural* religion lies level to the meanest capacity; for all men, however employed in the world, are capable of being convinced that there is a God who governs the world; and they feel themselves to be of a moral nature and accountable creatures.   And as *Christianity* entirely falls in

[*] Daniel, xii., 10. See also Is., xxix., 13, 14; Mat., vi., 23, and xi., 25, and xiii., 11, 12; John, iii., 19, and v., 44; 1 Cor., ii., 14; 2 Cor., iv., 4; 2 Tim., iii., 13; and that affectionate, as well as authoritative admonition, so very many times inculcated, *He that hath ears to hear let him hear.* Grotius saw so plainly the thing intended in these and other passages of Scripture of the like sense, as to say that the proof given of Christianity was less than it might have been for this very purpose. " Ut ita sermo Evangelii tanquam lapis esset Lydius ad quem ingenia sanabilia explorarentur."—*Butler.*

[†] The *internal* evidence of religion seems chiefly to have been intended as a means of moral probation. *Vide* John, vii., 17.

with this natural sense of things, so they may be persuaded and made to see that there is evidence of miracles wrought in attestation of it, and many appearing completions of prophecy. But though this general proof be liable to objections, and run up into difficulties which can not be answered so as to satisfy curiosity, yet we can see that the proof is not lost in these difficulties, or destroyed by these objections. It is true, this requires *knowledge, time, and attention*, and therefore can not be the business of every man; but it ought to be considered by such as have picked up objections from others, and take for granted upon their authority that they are of weight against revelation, or by often retailing them, fancy they see that they are of weight. In this, as in all other matters, doubtfulness, ignorance, or error must attend the neglect of the *necessary* means of information.

IV. *Analogy objected against the fitness of the evidence of Revelation.* "If a prince or common master were to send directions to a servant, he would take care that they should always bear the certain marks of him from whom they came, and that their sense should always be plain; so that there should be no possible doubt, concerning their authority or meaning."

ANSWER. The proper answer to all this kind of objections is, that wherever the fallacy lies, it is even certain we can not argue thus with respect to

Q*

Him who is the Governor of the World, and particularly that he does not afford us such information, with respect to our temporal affairs and interests. However, there is a full answer to this objection, from the very nature of religion—for they are not *parallel* cases. The prince regards only the external event—the thing's being done ; religion regards the inward motive—and exercise by action. If the prince regarded the same, if he wished to prove the understanding or loyalty of a servant, he would not always give his orders in such a plain manner. It may be added, the Divine Will respecting morality and religion may be considered either absolute or conditional ; it can not be absolute in any other way than that we should act virtuously in such given circumstances, and not by His changing of our circumstances ; so that it is still in our power to do or contradict His will. But the whole constitution of nature affords certain instances of its being conditional, that if we act so or so, we shall be rewarded ; if otherwise, punished.

Several of these observations may well seem strange, perhaps unintelligible, to many good men ; but if the persons for whose sake they are made, think so—persons who object as above, and throw off all regard to religion under pretence of want of evidence, they are desired to consider whether their thinking so be owing to any thing unintelligible in these observations, or to their *not having such a sense of religion, as even their state of skepticism does in all reason require ?* It ought to be forced upon the reflection of these persons, that our nature and condition require us, in the daily course of life, to act upon evidence much lower than probable, and to engage in pursuits when the probability is greatly against success, if it be credible that possibly we may succeed in them.

QUESTIONS—CHAPTER VI.

1. Upon what *supposition* is the weak objection founded that "because revelation is left upon doubtful evidence it can not be true?" Give a general answer to it.

2. Explain in like manner the foundation of the 2d objection that "Revelation can not be true from its want of universality;" and answer it generally.

3. Give a *particular application* of the subject to the evidence of revealed religion in different ages, and the degrees of religious light enjoyed by various parts of mankind.

4. What considerations may tend to reconcile us to the *apparently* unequal dispensations of the Creator in regard to religion?

5. Admitting revelation to be uncertain in its evidence, there are three practical reflections which will tend to remove all causes of complaint. Name them.

6. How does Butler prove that there is not *a great* difference between what might in reason be the rule of life to those who really doubt, and those who are fully convinced of the truth of religion?

7. How does Butler prove that *doubting* necessarily implies *some degree* of evidence for that for which we doubt?

8. Show that the same account may be given of doubts in the evidence of religion as of temptation and difficulties in practice.

9. Give a summary of the argument in which it is explained, that *uncertainty* in religious truths may partly arise from our own neglect.

10. Answer the apparent analogy, by which an objection is raised against the fitness of revelation being left upon doubtful evidence.

CHAPTER VII.

OF THE PARTICULAR EVIDENCE FOR CHRISTIANITY.

The presumptions against Revelation, and objections against
the general scheme of Christianity, and particular things
relating to it being removed, there remains to be considered what positive evidence we have for its truth ; this is
considered under two heads.

I. The direct and fundamental evidence for Christianity from
Miracles and Prophecy, and various objections answered.

II. The *direct* and *circumstantial* evidence considered as
making up one argument.

WE proceed to consider what is the positive evidence for the truth of Christianity. We shall,
therefore, First, make some observations relating
to *miracles*, and the appearing completions of *prophecy*, (which are its fundamental proofs), and consider what analogy suggests in answer to the objections brought against this evidence; and, Secondly,
We shall endeavor to give some account of a general argument, consisting both of the *direct* and *collateral* evidence (for the latter ought never to be
urged apart from the former), considered as making
up one argument ; this being the kind of proof

upon which we determine most questions of difficulty concerning common facts, alleged to have happened, or seeming likely to happen, especially questions relating to conduct. The conviction arising from this kind of proof, may be compared to what they call the *effect* in architecture or other works of art—a result from a great number of things so and so disposed and taken into one view.

I. 1. *The Historical Evidence of Miracles.*

The Old Testament affords the same historical evidence of the miracles of Moses and of the Prophets, as of the common affairs of the Jewish nation.   And the Gospels and Acts afford the same historical evidence of the miracles and of the common facts—because they are alike related in *plain, unadorned narratives.*   Had the authors of these books appeared to aim at an entertaining manner of writing, the case would be different; then it might be said that the miracles were introduced, like poetic descriptions and prodigies, to animate a dull relation—to *amuse* the reader and engage his attention.

2. Some parts of Scripture, containing an account of miracles fully sufficient to prove the truth of Christianity, are quoted as authentic and genuine from the age in which they are said to be written, down to the present.

3. The miraculous history, *in general*, is confirmed—by the establishment of the Jewish and Christ-

ian religions; events cotemporary with the miracles related to be wrought in attestation of both, or subsequent to them. These miracles are a satisfactory account of those events, of *which no other satisfactory account can be given, nor any account at all* but what is merely imaginary and invented. Mere guess, supposition, and possibility, when opposed to historical evidence, prove nothing, but that historical evidence is not demonstrative. There must be something *positive* alleged against the proof of the genuineness and authenticity of Scripture, before it can be invalidated; either that this evidence may be confronted by historical evidence on the other side, or the general incredibility of the things related, or inconsistency in the general turn of history; none of which can be proved.

4. The Epistles of St. Paul, from the nature of epistolary writing, and moreover, from several of them being written, not to particular individuals, but to Churches, carry in them evidences of their being genuine, beyond what can be in a mere historical narrative, left to the world at large. One Epistle especially, which is chiefly referred to here (the 1st to the Corinthians), has a distinct and particular evidence, from the manner in which it is quoted by Clemens Romanus, in an epistle of his own to that Church. Indeed, the testimony of St. Paul is to be considered as detached from that of the rest of the Apostles, for the author declares,

in his Epistles, that he received the Gospel in general, and the institution of the Communion in particular, not from the rest of the Apostles, or jointly together with them, but *alone and from Christ himself;* and he declares farther, that he was endued with the power of working miracles, as what was publicly known to those very people, in the manner any one would speak to another of a thing which was as familiar, and as much known in common to them both, as any thing in the world.* This evidence, joined with what these Epistles have in common with the rest of the New Testament, does not leave a *particular* pretence for denying their genuineness: for, as to *general doubts* concerning it, any single fact, of such kind and antiquity, may have them, from the very nature of human affairs and human testimony.

5. It is an acknowledged historical fact, that Christianity offered itself to the world, and demanded to be received, upon the *allegation* of miracles, publicly wrought to attest the truth of it, in such an age, and that it was actually received by great numbers in that very age, and upon the professed belief of the reality of these miracles. Now all this is peculiar to the Jewish and Christian dispensations. Mohammedism was not introduced on the

* *Vide* Rom., xv., 19; 1 Cor., xii., 8, 9, 10—28, &c., and xiii., 1, 2, 8, and the whole of xiv.; 2 Cor., xii., 12, 13; Gal., iii., 25.

ground of miracles, *i. e.*, public ones, for as revelation itself is miraculous, all pretence to it must necessarily imply some pretence to miracles.* Particular institutions in Paganism or Popery, *confirmed* by miracles after they were established, or even supposed to be *introduced* and believed on the ground of miracles, are not parallel instances, for single things of this kind are easily accounted for, after parties are formed, and have power in their hands—when the leaders of them are in veneration with the multitude, and political interests are blended with religious claims and religious distinctions. But even if this be not admitted to be *peculiar* to Christianity, the *fact* is admitted that it was professed to be believed on the evidence of miracles. Now, certainly it is not to be supposed that such numbers of men, in the most distant parts of the world should forsake the religion of their country, and embrace another which could not but expose them to much self-denial, and, indeed, must have been a giving up of the world in a great degree, unless they were really convinced of the truth of these miracles, as they professed, when they became Christians, and this their testimony is the

* This was all that Mohammed pretended to. "The *Koran itself* is a miracle." So far was he from claiming to himself the working of *public* miracles, that he declared he did *not* work them, since those wrought by others, the Prophets, Apostles, and Jesus Christ, failed to bring conviction with them!—*Vide Sale's Koran, passim.*

R

same kind of evidence for those miracles as if they had written it, and their writings had come down to us.   And it is *real* evidence, because it is of *facts* of which they had capacity and full opportunity to inform themselves.   It is also distinct from the direct historical evidence, though of the same kind ; for the general belief of any fact at the time in which it is said to have happened, is distinct from the express testimony of the historian.   We admit the credulity of mankind ; but we should not forget their suspicions, and backwardness even to *believe*, and greater still to *practice*, what makes against their interest.   So that the conversion of many to Christianity, when *education, prejudice* and *authority* were against it, is an undoubted presumption of its Divine origin.   It lies with unbelievers to show why such evidence as all this amounts to, is not to be credited.*   Accordingly, there is

OBJECTED. 1st. "Numberless enthusiastic, people, in different ages and countries expose them-

---

* If it be objected that it is rather slender ground upon which to stand, merely that *we cannot prove the contrary, or the falsehood* of the thing, we may answer, that it is not intended to be ground to *rest on;* it is intended to set us in motion ; and the evidence will grow in proportion to the earnestness and sincerity to ascertain the point.   Now, is there not a moral fitness in this, that evidence should be progressive, and that in proportion to the singleness of eye and the diligence with which it is sought and investigated ?— *Wolfe's Remains.*

selves to the same difficulties which the primitive Christians did, and are ready to give up their lives for the most idle follies imaginable."

ANSWER. Though testimony is no proof of enthusiastic opinions, or of any opinions at all, yet (as is allowed in all other cases) it is a proof of facts. The Apostles' sufferings proved *their belief* of the facts; and their belief proved the facts, for they were such as came under the observation of their senses.

2d OBJECTION. " But enthusiasm greatly *weakens*, if it does not totally and absolutely *destroy*, the evidence of testimony even for *facts*, in matters relating to religion.

ANSWER. If great numbers of men, not appearing in any peculiar degree weak or negligent, affirm that they saw and heard such things plainly with their eyes and ears, and are admitted to be in earnest, such testimony is evidence of the strongest kind we can have for any matter of fact. Such an account of their testimony must be admitted, in place of that far-fetched, indirect, and wonderful one of enthusiasm, until *some incredibility can be shown in the things thus attested, or contrary testimony produced.* The very mention of enthusiasm goes upon this previous supposition, which must be proved before such a charge need be answered; but as the *contrary* has been proved, an answer to it is much less required. However, as religion is supposed to be peculiarly liable to enthusiasm, we will consider what analogy suggests.   Nameless and numberless prejudices, romance, affectation, humor, a desire to engage attention or to surprise, party spirit, custom, little competition, unaccountable likings and dislikings, are to be considered as influences of a like kind to enthusiasm, because they are often scarce known or reflected upon by the persons themselves who are influenced by them. These influence men strongly in *common* matters, yet *human testimony* in these matters is naturally and justly believed notwithstanding.

3d OBJECTION. " But the primitive Christians might still, *in part*, be deceived themselves, and, *in part*, designedly impose upon others, which is rendered very credible from that mixture of real enthusiasm and real knavery to be met with in the same characters."

ANSWER. It is a fact that, though endued with reason to distinguish truth from falsehood, and also with regard to truth in what they say, men are all liable to be deceived by prejudice ; and there are persons who, from their regard to truth, would not invent a lie entirely without any foundation at all, but yet would propagate it after it is once invented, with heightened circumstances. And others, though they would not *propagate* a lie, yet, which is a lower degree of falsehood, will let it pass without contradiction.   This is analogical to the ground of the objection; yet, notwithstanding all this, human testimony remains still a natural ground of assent, and this assent a natural principle of action.

4th OBJECTION.   But it is a *fact* that mankind have, in different ages, been strangely deluded with pretences to miracles and wonders."

ANSWER. They have been, by no means, oftener, nor are they more liable to be, deceived by these pretences than by others.*

5th OBJECTION.   But there is *a very considerable degree of historical evidence* for miracles acknowledged to be fabulous."

ANSWER. Is there *the like* evidence?   By no means.†   But, even admitting that there were, the consequence would not be that the evidence of the latter is not to be admitted; for what would such a conclusion really amount to but this, that evidence confuted by contrary evidence, or any way overbalanced, destroys the credibility of other evidence neither confuted nor overbalanced?   If two men, of equally good reputation, had given evi-

---

* *Counterfeit coin* supposes that there is such a thing in the world as good money, and no one would pretend *outwardly to be virtuous,* unless some were really so. In the same manner, false miracles suppose the existence of real ones; and the cheats that have been imposed upon the world, far from furnishing us with reasons to reject all miracles in general, are, on the contrary, a strong proof that *some,* of which they are imitations, have been genuine.—*Douglas on Miracles.*

† *Vide* Paley's Evidences, Part 2, where this point is satisfactorily proved.

R*

dence in different cases no way connected, and one of them had been convicted of perjury, would this confute the testimony of the other ?

In addition to all these answers, it may be observed, it can never be sufficient to overthrow direct historical evidence, indolently to say, that there are so many principles from whence men are liable to be deceived themselves, and disposed to deceive others, especially in matters of religion, that one knows not what to believe. It, indeed, *weakens* the evidence of testimony in all cases, and it will appear to do so in different degrees according to men's experience or notions of hypocrisy or enthusiasm ; but nothing can *destroy* the evidence of testimony in any case, but a proof or probability that persons are not competent judges of the facts to which they give testimony, or that they are actually under some indirect influence in giving it, in such particular case. Till this be made out, the *natural* laws of human actions require that testimony be admitted. Now, the first and most obvious presumption is, that they could not be deceived themselves, nor would deceive others ; for the importance of Christianity must have engaged the attention of its first converts, so as to have rendered them less liable to be deceived from carelessness, than they would in common matters ; and the strong obligations to veracity which their religion laid them under made them less liable to deceive others. The external evidence for Christianity, unbelievers, who know any thing at all of the matter, must admit; that is, as persons in many cases own they see strong evidence from testimony for the truth of things which yet they can not be convinced are true—supposing that there is contrary testimony, or that the things are incredible. But there is no testimony contrary to that which we have been considering; and it has been fully proved that there is no incredibility in Christianity in general, or in any part of it.

I. 2d. *The evidence of Christianity from Prophecy.* The obscurity or unintelligibleness of one part of a prophecy, whether it arise from the nature of prophecy or from want of learning or of opportunities of inquiry, or from the deficiencies in civil history, and the different accounts of historians, does not, in any degree, invalidate the proof of foresight arising from the clear fulfillment of those parts which are understood. For the case is evidently the same as if those parts which are not understood were lost, or not written at all, or written in an unknown tongue. Suppose a writing partly in cipher and partly in plain words at length, and that in the part understood there appeared mention of several known facts; it would never come into any man's thoughts to imagine, that, if he understood the whole, perhaps he might find that those facts were not in reality known by the writer.

The fulfillment of the facts known is extensive enough to prove foresight more than human.

1st OBJECTION. "Considering each prophecy distinctly, it does not at all appear that the prophecies were intended of those particular events to which they are applied by Christians; and, therefore, if they mean any thing, they are intended of other events unknown to us, and not of these at all."

ANSWER. A long series of prophecy being applicable to such and such events, is itself a proof that it referred to them. This appears from analogy; for there are two kinds of writing which bear a great resemblance to prophecy, with respect to the matter before us—the mythological, and satirical where the satire is, to a certain degree, concealed. In the *former* kind, a man might be assured that he understood what an author intended by a fable or parable, related without any application or moral, merely from seeing it to be easily capable of such application, and that such a moral might naturally be deduced from it. And, in a *satirical* writing, he might be fully assured that such persons and events were intended, merely from its being applicable to them; and his satisfaction that he understood the *intended* meaning of these writings would be greater or less, in proportion as he saw the general turn of them and the number of particular things to be capable of such application.

In the same way, if a long series of prophecy is applicable to the present state of the Church, and to the political situations of the kingdoms of the world, some thousand years after these prophecies were delivered; and if a long series of prophecy, delivered before the coming of Christ, is applicable to Him, these things are in themselves a proof that the prophetic history was intended of Him, and of those events, in proportion as the general turn of it, and the number and variety of particular prophecies are capable of such application. And although the appearing fulfillment of prophecy is to be allowed to determine its meaning, it may be added that prophecies have been determined *beforehand*, as they have been fulfilled. The prophecies of a Messiah were applied to Him, by the Jews, before the coming of Christ; and those concerning the state of the Church in the last ages, were applied to it by the primitive Christians, as the event seems to verify.

Farther, even if it could be shown, to a high degree of probability, that the Prophets thought of events different from those which Christians allege to be the completion of their predictions; or that their prophecies are capable of being applied to other events than what Christians apply them to; yet to say that the Scriptures, and the things contained in them, can have no other or farther meaning than those persons thought or had, who first recited or wrote them, is evidently saying that those persons were the original, proper, and sole authors of these books, and not the amanuenses of the Holy Ghost; which is absurd, while the authority of these books is under consideration—it is begging the question.   If we knew the whole meaning of the *compiler* of a book, taken from memoirs, for instance, we would not suppose that we knew, from this, the whole meaning of the *author* of the memoirs.   So that the question is, whether a series of prophecy has been fulfilled, in any real sense of the words : for such completion is equally a proof of foresight, more than human, whether the Prophets are or are not *supposed* to have understood it in a different sense.   For, though it is clear that the Prophets did not understand the full meaning of their predictions, it is another question how far they *thought* they did, and in *what sense* they understood them.   So that it is useless to show that prophecy is applicable to events of the age in which it was written, or of ages before it.   To have proved this, *before* the completion, might, indeed, have answered some purpose; for it might have prevented the expectation of any such farther completion.   For example, if Porphyry could have shown that some principal parts of the book of Daniel, for instance the 7th verse of the 7th chapter, which the Christians interpreted of the latter ages, was applicable to events which happened before, or about, the age

of Antiochus Epiphanes,* this might have prevented
them from expecting any farther completion of it.
But even if he could prove his assertion—which by
no means appears—these remarks show it to be of
no consequence: and they are remarks which must
be acknowledged, by those of a fair mind, to be
just, and the evidence referred to in them real.
But it is much more easy, and more falls in with
the negligence, presumption, and willfulness of the
generality, to determine at once, with a decisive air
—there is nothing in them.

II. We shall now endeavor to give some account
of the general argument for the truth of Christianity; consisting both of the direct and circumstantial evidence, considered as making up one argument, for three reasons—1st, this is the kind of
evidence upon which most questions of difficulty,
in common practice, are determined—evidence
arising from various coincidences, which support
and confirm each other; 2d, this seems to be of
the greatest importance, and not duly attended to

---

* It appears that Porphyry did nothing, worth mentioning,
in this way.   For Jerome, on the passage, says: "Duas pos-
teriores bestias in uno Macedonum regno ponit."   And as to
the ten kings, "Decem reges enumerat, qui fuerunt sævissi-
mi: ipsosque reges non unius ponit regni, verbi gratia, Mace-
doniæ, Syriæ, Asiæ, et Egypti, sed de diversis regnis unum
efficit regum ordinem."   And in this way of interpretation
any thing may be made of any thing.—*Vide Newton on the
Prophecies, and Bishop Chandler's Vindication of Christianity.*

by every one; 3d, the matters of fact here enu-
merated, being acknowledged by unbelievers, the
weight of the whole, collectively, must be ackowl-
edged to be very important.

(1.) Revelation, whether real or supposed, may
be considered as wholly historical—for *prophecy* is
nothing but anticipated history—and doctrines and
precepts are matters of fact.   The general design of
Scripture, containing this revelation, thus considered as historical, may be said to be, to give us an
account of the world in one single view as God's
World; by which it appears distinguished from
all other books.   It begins with an account of
God's creation of the world, in order to ascertain
by what He has done, the object of our worship,
distinct from idols, and the Being of whom the
whole volume treats.   St. John, perhaps in allusion
to this, *begins* his gospel with an account of Him
by whom God created all things.   It contains an
abridgment of the history of the world, in the view
just mentioned, from the first transgression, during
the continuance of its apostacy from God, till the
*times of the restitution of all things ;** giving a general account of the governments by which religion
is, has been, or shall be affected.   On this it may
be remarked, *that the supposed doubtfulness of the*
evidence for revelation, in place of implying a posi-

* Acts, iii., 21.   *Vide,* also Rev., x., 7 ; Dan., ii., 44, vii.,
22 ; Rev., xxii., 5 ; Dan., vii., 27.

tive argument that it is NOT *true, implies a positive argument that it is* TRUE : for, if any common relation of such *antiquity*, such *extent*, and *variety* could be proposed to the examination of the world, and if it could not be confuted in any age of knowledge and liberty, to the satisfaction of reasonable men, this would be thought a strong presumptive proof of its truth ; strong in proportion to the probability that if it were false, it might have been shown to be so.   Now Christianity is not said, by any, to have been thus confuted.   Farther, the Old Testament, together with the moral system of the world, contains a chronological account of the beginning of it ; and, from thence, an unbroken genealogy of mankind for many ages before common history begins.   It contains an account of God's making a covenant with a particular nation—His government of them—His threatenings " that he would scatter them among all people, from one end of the earth unto the other"—and His promise " that he would bring again the captivity of His people Israel, and plant them upon their land—and they should be no more pulled up out of the land."*
It foretells that God would raise them up a particular person—the Messiah—in whom all His promises should be finally fulfilled ; and consequently (as profane, as well as sacred, history informs us),

---

* *Vide* Deut., xxx., 2, 3; Is., xlv., 17, lx., 21; Jer., xxx., 11, xlvi., 28; Amos, ix., 15; Jer. xxxi., 36.

S

there was a general expectation of his appearing
at such a particular time, before any one appeared
claiming to be that person.   It foretells also, that
he should be rejected by those to whom he was so
long promised,* and that he should be the Saviour
of the Gentiles.†   The Scripture farther informs us,
that at the time the Messiah was expected, a person arose in this nation claiming to be that Messiah,
to whom all the prophecies referred.   He continued
some years working miracles, and endued his disciples with a power of doing the same, to be a
proof of the truth of that religion which He commis-
sioned them to publish; that they, accordingly, made
numerous converts, and established His religion in
the world; to the end of which the Scripture pro-
fesses to give a prophetic account of the state of
this religion among mankind.

(2.) Suppose now a person, quite ignorant of history, to remark these things in Scripture, without
knowing but that the whole was a late fiction; then
to be informed of the following confessed facts:
that the profession and establishment of natural religion is greatly owing to this book, and the sup-

---

* *Vide* Is., viii., 14, 15, xlix., 5, xliii.; Mal., i., 10, 11,
and iii.

† Is., xlix., 6, ii., xi., lvi., 7; Mal., i., 11.   To which must
be added the other prophecies of the like kind, several in the
New Testament, and very many in the Old, which describe
what shall be the completion of the revealed plan of Providence.

posed revelation which it contains,* even in those
countries which do not acknowledge the proper
authority of Scripture ; yet that it is acknowledged
by many nations—that religion is highly important (all this, considered together, would make
the appearing and receiving of this book seem the
most important event in the history of mankind, and
would claim for it, as if by a voice from heaven, a
serious examination) ; that the first parts of Scripture are acknowledged to be of the earliest antiquity ; that its chronology, and *common* history, are
entirely credible, being confirmed by the natural
and civil history of the world, collected from common historians, from the state of the earth, and
from the late inventions of arts and sciences ; that
there appears nothing related as done in any age,
not conformable† to the manners of that age ; that
there are all the internal marks imaginable of REAL

* But it is to be remembered, that how much soever the
establishment of natural religion in the world is owing to
Scripture-revelation, this does not destroy the proof of religion from reason, any more than the proof of *Euclid's Elements* is destroyed by a man's knowing, or thinking, that he
should never have seen the truth of the several propositions
contained in it, nor had those propositions come into his
thoughts, but for that mathematician.— *Butler.*

† There are several objections to passages of Scripture, occasioned by not considering them in reference to the manners of the times. Thus it appears that the things objected
to, like many others that are censured in Christianity, and in
Scripture, are, in a greater or less degree, actual *proofs* of
their truth and authenticity.

characters ; that the *miracles* are interwoven with the *common* history—which, therefore, gives some credibility to them—that the Jews, of whom it chiefly treats, are acknowledged to have been an ancient nation, and divided from all others ; that they preserved natural religion among them, which can not be said of the Gentile world—(which again adds a credibility to the miracles, for they alone can satisfactorily account for this event) ; that as there was a national expectation among them,* raised from the prophecies of a Messiah to appear at such a time, so one at this time appeared claiming to be that Messiah ; that he was rejected by this nation (as seemed to be foretold), but received by the Gentiles, yet not upon the evidence of prophecy, but of miracles ; that the religion he taught supported itself under the greatest difficulties, gained ground, and at length became the religion of the world ; that, in the mean time, the Jewish polity was utterly destroyed, and the nation dispersed

---

* *Vide* Bishop Chandler's Vindication of Christianity, where it is fully proved that this expectation was general among the Jews and Samaritans. The effects of it may be judged from its extension among the Gentiles. To say nothing of the Arabians and of the appearing of the star to the Magi— Suetonius informs us (Vespasian, cap. iv., 8), " *Percrebuerat* oriente toto vetus et constans opinio, esse in fatis, ut eo tempore Judæâ profecti rerum potirentur." And Tacitus, in his history (lib. v., cap. 9), testifies, that " *Pluribus* persuasio inerat, antiquis sacerdotum literis contineri, eo ipso tempore fore, valesceret oriens, profectique Judæâ rerum potirentur."

over the face of the earth ; that, notwithstanding
this, they have remained a distinct numerous people
for so many centuries, even to this day ; which,
not only appears to be the express completion of
several prophecies concerning them, but also renders it, as one may say, a visible and easy possibility that the promises made to them, as a nation,
may yet be fulfilled ; that there are obvious appearances of the state of the world in other respects,
besides what relates to the Jews, and of the Christian Church having so long answered, and still answering to the prophetic history.   Let him view
these *acknowledged facts* in connection with what
has been before collected from Scripture, and the
weight must appear very considerable to any reasonable mind.

OBJECTIONS PRECLUDED : All these things, and
the several particulars contained under them, require to be distinctly and most thoroughly exam-
ined.   This has not been attempted here.   However, the things advanced, must be acknowledged
by unbelievers ; for though they may say that the
historical evidence of miracles, wrought in attestation of Christianity, is not sufficient to convince
them that such miracles were really wrought, they
can not deny that there is such historical evidence,
it being a known matter of fact that there is.   They
object to the appearance of a standing miracle, in
the Jews remaining a distinct people in their dis-

persion, accounting for this fact by their religion forbidding them intermarriages with those of any other, and prescribing them a great many peculiarities in their food, which prevent them being incorporated with any other people. But an event, considered apart from all coincidence, may not appear miraculous, yet the coincidence with prophecy may be so, though the event itself be supposed not. Thus the concurrence of our Saviour's being born at Bethlehem, with a long series of prophecy and other coincidences, is doubtless miraculous, though the event itself—his birth at that place, appears to have been brought about in a *natural* way, of which, however, no one can be certain. Men may say, the conformity betwen the prophecies and events is by accident; but there are many instances in which such *conformity* itself can not be denied. They may say, with regard to such kind of collateral things as those above mentioned, that any odd accidental events, without meaning, will have a meaning found in them by fanciful people. Men, I say, may talk thus, but no one who is serious can possibly think these things to be nothing, if he considers the importance of collateral things, and even of lesser circumstances, in the evidence of *probability*, as distinguished in nature from the evidence of *demonstration*. This general view of evidence may induce serious persons to set down every thing, which they think may be of any

real weight at all in proof of it, and particularly
the many seeming completions of prophecy. Nor
should I dissuade any one from setting down what
he thought made for the contrary side ; but let him
remember that a mistake on one side may be, in
its consequences, much more dangerous than a
mistake on the other ; but is not this prejudice ?
If suffered to influence the judgment,* it is so indeed, and, like other prejudices, it operates contrary ways in different men ; for some are inclined
to believe what they hope, and others what they
fear ; and it is manifest unreasonableness to apply
to men's *passions* in order to gain their *assent*. But,
in deliberations concerning *conduct*, there is nothing which reason more requires to be taken into
the account than the *importance* of it. But the
truth of our religion, like the truth of common facts,
is to be judged by all the evidence taken together.
And, unless the whole series of things which may
be alleged in this argument, and every particular

---

* Thus, though it is indeed absurd to talk of the greater
merit of assent upon little or no evidence than upon demonstration, yet the strict discharge of our duty with less sensible
evidence, does imply in it a better character than the same
diligence in the discharge of it upon more sensible evidence.
This fully accounts for, and explains, that assertion of our
Saviour—" *Blessed are they that have not seen and yet have
believed*"—have become Christians, and obeyed the Gospel,
upon less sensible evidence than that which Thomas, to
whom he is speaking, insisted upon.—*Butler's Sermon on the
Ignorance of Man.*

thing in it, can reasonably be supposed to have been by accident (for here the stress of the argument for Christianity lies), then is the truth of it proved ; in like manner as, if in any common case, numerous events acknowleged were to be alleged in proof of any other event disputed, the truth of *this* event would be proved, not only if any one of the acknowledged ones did of itself clearly imply it, but though no one of them singly did so, if the whole of the acknowledged events taken together could not, in reason, be supposed to have happened, unless the disputed ones were true.*

---

* The evidences of religion being so exceedingly dissimilar are highly characteristic of its truth. If man's contrivance, or if the favor of accidents, *could* have given to Christianity any of its apparent testimonies—either its miracles or its prophecy, its morals or its propagation, or, if I may so speak, its Founder—there could be no room to believe, nor even to imagine, that all these appearances of great credibility could be united together by any such causes. If a successful craft could have contrived its public miracles, or so much as the pretence of them, it required another reach of craft and new resources to provide and adapt its prophecies to the same object. Further, it demanded not only a different art, but a totally opposite character, to conceive and promulgate its admirable morals. Again, the achievement of its propagation in defiance of the powers and terrors of the world—but the hypothesis sinks under its incredibility. For, *each* of these suppositions of contrivance being arbitrary, as it certainly is, and unsupported, the *climax* of them is an extravagance ; and if the imbecility of *art* is foiled in the hypothesis, the combinations of *accident* are too vain to be thought of.—*Davison on Prophecy.*

It is obvious how much advantage the nature
of this evidence gives to those persons who attack
Christianity, *especially in conversation.*   For it is
easy to show, in a short and lively manner, that
such and such things are liable to objection—that
this and another thing is of little weight in itself—
but impossible to show, in like manner, the united
force of the whole argument in one view.

QUESTIONS—CHAPTER VII.

1. In what does Butler proceed to consider the *positive* evidence for the truth of Christianity?

2. Give summarily the five heads under which Butler treats of the historical evidence of miracles.

3. Why must peculiar importance be attached to the testimony afforded by the writings of St. Paul?

4. State the argument which leads to the conclusion that "the conversion of many to Christianity, when *education, prejudice,* and *authority* were against it, is an undoubted presumption of its Divine origin."

5. Answer the objection, that "*Enthusiasm* greatly weakens, if not destroys, the credibility of evidence given even for *facts,* in matters relating to religion."

6. How may we answer the assertion that "there is a considerable degree of historical evidence for miracles acknowledged to be fabulous?"

7. What *general* answer may be given to *all* the *foregoing* objections against evidences of religion, taken from the liability of men to be deceived?

8. In stating the evidence of Christianity derived from prophecies, how does Butler excuse the defects imputed to them, from the alleged obscurity of certain parts in them?

9. Answer the objection, that "Considering *each* prophecy *distinctly,* it does not at all appear that the prophecies were intended for those particular events to which they are applied by Christians."

10. Explain why we may reasonably assert, that "It is useless (for a person arguing against the truth of prophecy) to show that prophecy is *applicable* to events of the age in which it was written." Also give

Butler's remarks in conclusion of this part of the chapter.

11. When considering *both* the *direct* and *circumstantial* evidence for the truth of Christianity, as making up *one* argument, in what light may Scriptural revelation be looked upon? What is its general design? And how does the *supposed doubtfulness* of evidence bear upon the question of its genuineness?

12. Give a summary of the *acknowledged facts*, which, in *connection* with what is collected from the Old Testament respecting its ancient chronology, the history of Israel, prophecies of Christ; or from the New, respecting the Gospel History or prophecies, *ought* to have great weight with a reasonable and impartial *inquirer*.

13. Mention some of the specious reasonings by which unbelievers endeavor to evade the force of the above arguments; and answer them.

14. Prove the reasonableness of the following warning, given to a man noting down every thing which seems to be a proof *against* religion, "Let him remember that a mistake on one side may be, in its consequences, much more dangerous than a mistake on the other."

15. Taking it as an admitted principle, that the truth of our religion, as of other common facts, is to be judged by all the evidence taken together, show where the *stress* of the argument for Christianity lies.

16. Describe the argument given by Davison, to show that the evidences of religion being so exceedingly *dissimilar*, are highly characteristic.

CHAPTER VIII.

OF THE OBJECTIONS WHICH MAY BE MADE AGAINST
ARGUING FROM THE ANALOGY OF NATURE TO RE-
LIGION.

I. The Objections that may be urged against arguing from
Analogy to Religion may be answered, in general, by saying that they are owing to half views—to indeterminate
language, and the deficiencies and abuse of words; but
each objection can be separately precluded.

II. This Treatise proceeds upon the *principles of others*, and,
therefore, is not as full a confirmation of Religion as it
might otherwise be.

I. 1st. OBJECTED. " IT is a *poor thing* to solve
difficulties in revelation by saying, that there are
the same in natural religion, when what is wanting
is to clear both of them of these their *common*, as
well as others their *respective*, difficulties."

ANSWER. The having all difficulties cleared, may
be the same as requiring to comprehend the Divine
Nature, and the whole plan of Providence. As to
its being a *poor* thing to argue from natural to revealed religion, it has always been allowed, and it
is often necessary to argue in such a way of probable deduction from what is acknowledged to what
is disputed; and, indeed, the epithet *poor* is as

properly applicable to the whole of human life. Is it not a *poor* thing, for instance, that even the most eminent physician should have so little knowledge in the cure of diseases as often to act upon conjecture, where the life of a man is concerned? Yet it is not a poor thing in comparison of having no skill at all. Farther, it is of *great consequence* to show that objections urged against revelation are as much leveled against natural religion; for thus we prove that the objectors are arguing against moral Providence, while they seem, whether intentionally or not, to argue against revelation; for nothing more has been taken for granted in the second part of this treatise than there was in the first, viz., the existence of an Author of nature; so that Christianity is vindicated, not from its analogy to *natural religion*, but chiefly from its analogy to the constitution of nature.

2d. OBJECTED. "It is a strange way of convincing men of the obligations of religion, to show them that they have as little reason for their worldly pursuits."

ANSWER. Religion is a practical thing, and consists in such a determinate course of life, as there is reason to think is commanded by the Author of nature, and will, upon the whole, be our happiness under His government. Now, if men can be convinced that they have the like reason to believe this as to believe that care of their temporal affairs

T

will be their advantage—this, with the infinitely
superior interest which religion proposes, will be
an argument for the practice of it.   But the chief
and proper force of the argument, referred to in
the objection, lies in another place; for it is said,
that the proof of religion is involved in such inex-
tricable difficulties as to render it doubtful; and
this is made a positive argument against its truth,
since, if it were true, it is said to be incredible that
it should be left to doubtful evidence.   Now, the
observation, that, from the natural constitution of
things, we must, in our temporal concerns, almost
continually, and in matters of great consequence,
act upon evidence of a like kind and degree to the
evidence of religion, is an answer to this argument,
because it is a general instance made up of numerous particular ones of somewhat in the conduct
of the Author of nature toward us similar to what
is said to be incredible.

3d Objection. "It is a strange way of vindi-
cating the justice and goodness of the Author of
nature, and of removing objections against both, to
which the system of religion lies open, to show
that the like objections lie against natural Providence.   This is a way of answering objections
against religion without even pretending to make
out that the system of it, or the particular things
in it objected against, are *reasonable;* especially
when it is admitted that analogy is no answer to

such objections, *i. e.*, those against wisdom, justice, and goodness."

ANSWER. The design of this treatise is, not to vindicate the character of God, but to show the obligations of men—not to justify his Providence, but to show us our duty. For, 1st, It is not necessary to justify the dispensations of Providence against objections, any further than to show, that the things objected to may be consistent with, and even instances of justice and goodness, as has been already shown (Chap. 4, Part II.). 2d. The objections are not endeavored to be removed, by showing that the like objections, *allowed to be conclusive*, lie against natural Providence; but these objections being shown to be *inconclusive*, the credibility of the things objected against, considered as matters of fact, is shown from their conformity to the constitution of nature. 3d. This would be of weight, even though these objections were not answered. For, there being the proof of religion, above set down, and religion implying several *facts* —for instance, the fact that God will hereafter reward and punish men for their actions—the observation, that His present government is by rewards and punishments, shows that *future fact* not to be incredible. 4th. Though objections against the *reasonableness* of the system of religion, can not be answered without entering into the consideration of its reasonableness; yet objections against the *credibility or truth* of the system may; because the system of it is reducible into matter of fact, and the probable truth of facts may be shown without considering their reasonableness. Nor is it *necessary* to prove the reasonableness of every precept and dispensation; though, in some cases, it is highly useful to do so. But the general obligations of religion are made out by proving the reasonableness of its *practice*. 5th. Though analogy be not an immediate answer to such objections, yet it is an immediate answer to what is intended by them, which is—to show that the things objected against are incredible.

4th. OBJECTED. " When analogical reasoning is carried to the utmost length, it will yet leave the mind in a very unsatisfied state."

ANSWER. It is acknowledged that the foregoing treatise is far from satisfactory ; but so would any natural institution of life appear, if reduced into a system, together with its evidence. Indeed, the unsatisfactory nature of the evidence on which we are obliged to act, in the daily course of life, is scarce to be expressed. Yet men do not throw away life, or disregard the interests of it, upon account of this doubtfulness. The evidence of religion, then, being admitted real, those who object against it, as not satisfactory, *i. e.*, as not being what they wish it, plainly forget the very *condition of our being ;* for satisfaction, in this sense, does not belong to such a creature as man. They also forget the very *notion of religion ;* for religion presupposes, in all those who will embrace it, a certain degree of integrity and honesty, just as much as speaking to a man presupposes that he understands the language in which you speak, or the warning a man of danger presupposes in him self-concern. And, therefore, the question is, not whether the evidence of religion be satisfactory as to the purposes of curiosity, but whether it be, in reason, sufficient to prove and discipline that virtue which it presupposes.

5th. OBJECTED. " It must be unaccountable ignorance of mankind, to imagine that men will be prevailed upon to forego their present interests and pleasures, from regard to religion, upon doubtful evidence."

ANSWER. Religion is intended for a trial and exercise of the morality of every person's character who *is* a subject of it ; and thus considered, it has its ends upon all persons to whom it has been proposed, with evidence sufficient in reason to influence their practice ; for it puts them in a state of probation, let them behave as they will in it. And the purpose of this treatise is to show how, in reason, men ought to behave—not how, in fact, they will behave. But the objection itself allows the things insisted upon in this treatise to be of *some* weight ; hence it is probable that the treatise

T

will have some influence; and this is the same reason in *kind*, though not in *degree*, to lay it before
men, as there would be if it were likely to have
a greater influence.

II. Thus the whole of the foregoing objections
arise in a great measure from half views, and un-
determinate language, but farther, it is to be observed, concerning them, that this treatise has proceeded upon the *principles of others* (*i. e.*, *notwithstanding* these principles—even admitting them to
be true).   Thus we have argued upon, or notwithstanding, the principles of Fatalists, which we do
not believe; and there have been omitted two
principles of the utmost importance, namely, the
abstract principles of liberty and moral fitness*—
which force themselves upon the mind, and in en-
deavoring to avoid them, the form of expression
sometimes made use of will appear strange, to such
as do not observe the reason of it.   Now these two
abstract principles being omitted, religion can only
be considered as a question of fact, and in this view

* Bishop Butler throughout the present work has only considered the *moral* difference, by which virtue and vice, as
such, are approved and disapproved.   Dr. Samuel Clarke,
has demonstrated (*vide* his sermons at Boyle's Lectures),
that there are essential differences in the qualities of human
actions established in nature, and this *natural* difference of
things, prior to and independent of all will, creates a natural
FITNESS in the agent to act agreeably to it: it is obvious that
the introduction of this principle would materially confirm
Bishop Butler's arguments.

it is here considered, since Christianity, and its
proof, are historical; and since also, natural religion is a matter of fact—as its general system is
contained in the fact, that there is a righteous Governor of the World. This may be considered apart
from these abstract principles; for instance, that
the three angles of a triangle *are equal* to two right
angles, may be considered apart from their *appearing so* to our minds; the former is an abstract
truth—the latter is only a matter of fact. So likewise, that there is in the nature of things an original standard of right and wrong, in actions, independent upon all will; but which unalterably
determines the will of God, to exercise the moral
government of finally righteous rewards and punishments—contains an abstract truth as well as matter of fact. But suppose that the government of
righteous rewards took place here—it would not
be an abstract truth, but only a matter of fact;
and the same questions as are now raised, might
still be raised about liberty and moral fitness; so
that this proof would remain, however the questions might be decided. And thus, God having
given mankind a moral faculty, the object of which
is actions, which naturally approves some actions
as of good desert, and condemns others as of ill
desert. This final righteous judgment is not to be
considered as an abstract truth, but as mere a fact
as if it took place here. This future fact has not,

indeed, been proved with the force with which it might be proved, by taking in the considerations of *liberty* and *moral fitness ;* but by omitting these, we have avoided the abstract questions concerning them, which have been perplexed with difficulties and abstruse reasonings; and we have confined ourselves to matter of fact, which must have been admitted, if any thing was, by those ancient skeptics, who would not have admitted abstract truth, but pretended to doubt whether there was any such thing as truth, or whether we could depend upon faculties for the knowledge of it in any case.

Hence, therefore, the force of this treatise may be distinctly observed. To such as are convinced of religion upon the proof of the two last-mentioned principles, it will be an additional proof and confirmation of it ; to such as are not satisfied with abstract reasonings, it will be an original proof of it. Those who believe will here find the scheme of Christianity cleared of objections, and its evidence peculiarly strengthened. Those who do not believe, will be shown the absurdity of all attempts to prove Christianity false, and they will also be shown its plain undoubted *credibility* at the least. Ridicule may be applied to show the *argument* from analogy in a disadvantageous light, but it is unquestionably a real one ; for, religion implying in it numerous *facts*, analogy being a confirmation of *all* facts to which it can be applied ; as it is the *only* proof of *most*, so it can not but be admitted by every one to be of considerable weight on the side of religion, both natural and revealed.

Conclusion.* Deduct, now, what is to be deducted from the positive evidence of religion, upon account of any weight which may be thought to remain in the objections against it upon the most skeptical principles, and the practical consequences will be—1st. That immorality is greatly aggravated in persons who have been made acquainted with Christianity : because the moral system of nature which Christianity lays before us, approves itself almost intuitively to a reasonable mind, upon seeing it proposed.   2d. That there is a middle, between a full satisfaction of the truth of Christianity, and a satisfaction of the contrary ; which middle state of mind consists in a serious, doubting apprehension, that it may be true : and this serious apprehension that Christianity may be true, lays persons under the strictest obligations of a serious regard to it throughout the whole of their life.   3d. It will appear that blasphemy and profaneness, with regard to Christianity, are without excuse ; for there is no temptation to it, but from the wantonness of vanity or mirth.   If this be a just account of things, and yet men can continue to vilify or

* The summaries prefixed to each chapter should now be read in continuation, as the force of the treatise consists in the whole analogy considered together.

disregard Christianity—which is to talk and act as if they had a demonstration of its falsehood—there is no reason to think they would alter their behavior to any purpose, though there were a demonstration of its truth.

QUESTIONS—CHAPTER VIII.

1. How may the objections urged against arguing from analogy to religion be *generally* answered?

2. Give a special reply to each of the following objections: 1st. What is wanted is, not to solve difficulties in revelation by saying that there are the *same* in *natural* religion, but to clear both of them of their *common* as well as their respective difficulties.

3. 2d Objection. It is a strange way of convincing men of the obligations of religion, to show them they have as *little reason* for their worldly pursuits.

4. 3d Objection. We can not vindicate the justice and goodness of the Author of nature, and remove objections against both, to which the system of nature is open, by showing that the like objections lie against natural Providence.

5. 4th Objection. Analogical reasoning, carried to the utmost extent, does not fully satisfy the mind.

6. 5th Objection. We can not imagine that men will forego their present interests and pleasures from regard to religion upon doubtful evidence.

7. Give an exposition of the argument, by which Butler distinguishes between *abstract* truths and matters of fact in religion. What important conclusion does he draw from thence?

8. To what purpose may the force of this whole treatise be effectually applied ?

9. Deducting every thing that can, upon skeptical principles, be required to be deducted from the positive evidence of religion, what practical consequences can be drawn from that which remains unassailable by sophistry and cavil ?

THE END.

VALUABLE STANDARD WORKS

IN THE SEVERAL DEPARTMENTS OF LITERATURE,

PUBLISHED BY

Harper & Brothers, New York.

Agriculture, Domestic Economy, &c

ARMSTRONG'S TREATISE ON AGRICULTURE: edited by BUEL
50 cents.
BEECHER'S (Miss C. E.) DOMESTIC ECONOMY, 75 cents.
———————————— HOUSEKEEPER'S RECEIPT-BOOK, 7
cents.
BROWNE'S TREES OF AMERICA, $5 00.
BUEL'S (JESSE) FARMER'S INSTRUCTOR, $1 00.
——— —— ———— FARMER'S COMPANION.
CHAPTAL'S CHEMISTRY APPLIED TO AGRICULTURE, 50 cts
COOK'S AMERICAN POULTRY BOOK, 35 cents.
GARDNER'S FARMER'S DICTIONARY. Engravings, $1 50.
GAYLORD AND TUCKER'S AMERICAN HUSBANDRY, $1 00.
KITCHINER'S COOK'S ORACLE AND HOUSEKEEPER'S MAN
UAL. 87½ cents.
MORRELL'S AMERICAN SHEPHERD. Plates. Paper, 75 cents
Muslin, 90 cents.
PARKES'S DOMESTIC DUTIES, FOR MARRIED LADIES, 75 cts
SMITH'S (Mrs.) MODERN AMERICAN COOKERY, 40 cents.
WEBSTER AND PARKES'S ENCYCLOPEDIA OF DOMESTIC
ECONOMY. Nearly 1000 Engravings. Muslin, $3 50. Sheep extra.
$3 75.

Biblical and Theological.

ABERCROMBIE'S MISCELLANEOUS ESSAYS, 37½ cents.
BAIRD'S (Dr.) VIEW OF RELIGION IN AMERICA, 62½ cents.
BARNES'S (ALBERT) NOTES ON THE NEW TESTAMENT, 6
vols., each volume sold separately, 75 cents.
QUESTIONS on the above, 6 vols., each 15 cents.
BELL'S (Sir CHARLES) MECHANISM OF THE HAND, 60 cents
BIBLICAL LEGENDS OF THE MUSSULMANS, 50 cents
BLAIR'S SERMONS, $1 50.
BONNECHOSE'S HISTORY OF THE EARLY REFORMERS, 40
cents.
BOOK OF COMMON PRAYER, corrected Standard Edition, in about
30 varieties of size and binding.
BROWN'S DICTIONARY OF THE HOLY BIBLE, $1 75.
——————— POCKET CONCORDANCE TO THE HOLY BIBLE,
37½ cents.
BUNYAN'S PILGRIM'S PROGRESS, 75 cents.
BUTLER'S ANALOGY OF NATURAL AND REVEALED RELIG
ION, 35 cents

CHALMERS ON THE POWER, WISDOM, AND GOODNESS OF
God in the Creation. 60 cents.
CHURCH (the) INDEPENDENT OF THE STATE, 90 cents.
COLTON ON THE RELIGIOUS STATE OF THE COUNTRY, 60
cents.
COMFORTER (the); OR, CONSOLATIONS FOR MOURNERS,
45 cents.
D'AUBIGNE'S DISCOURSES AND ESSAYS, 75 cents.
DAYS (the) OF QUEEN MARY, 25 cents.
DICK'S SIDEREAL HEAVENS, 45 cents.
———— CELESTIAL SCENERY; OR, PLANETARY SYSTEM,
45 cents.
DWIGHT'S (Rev. Dr.) THEOLOGY EXPLAINED AND DEFEND
ED. 4 vols., 8vo, $6 00.
GLEIG'S HISTORY OF THE BIBLE, 2 vols., 80 cents.
HALL'S (Rev. Robert) COMPLETE WORKS, 4 vols., $5 00.
HAWKS'S HISTORY OF THE PROT. EPISCOPAL CHURCH IN
Virginia, $1 75.
HOLY COAT (the) OF TREVES, 37½ cents.
HUNTER'S BIOGRAPHY OF THE PATRIARCHS, THE SAVIOR
&c., $1 75.
ILLUMINATED AND PICTORIAL BIBLE, 1600 Engravings, $22 50.
JARVIS'S (Rev. S. F.) CHRONOLOGICAL INTRODUCTION TO
THE History of the Church, $3 00.
JAY'S (Rev. William) COMPLETE WORKS, 3 vols., $5 00.
KEITH'S LAND OF ISRAEL, $1 25.
———— DEMONSTRATION OF CHRISTIANITY, $1 37½
———— ON THE PROPHECIES, 60 cents.
LE BAS'S LIFE OF WICLIF, 50 cents.
———— LIFE OF ARCHBISHOP CRANMER, $1 00.
MALAN. "CAN I JOIN THE CHURCH OF ROME WHILE MY
Rule of Faith is the Bible?" 25 cents.
MASON'S ZION'S SONGSTER, 25 cents.
M'ILVAINE'S (Bishop) EVIDENCES OF CHRISTIANITY, $1 00.
———— ON THE DANGERS OF THE CHURCH,
10 cents.
MILMAN'S (Rev. H. H.) HISTORY OF THE JEWS, 3 vols., $1 20
———— HISTORY OF CHRISTIANITY, $1 90.
MOSHEIM'S ECCLESIASTICAL HISTORY, by Murdock, $7 50
The same Work, by Maclaine, $3 50.
NEAL'S HISTORY OF THE PURITANS, 2 vols., $3 50.
PALEY'S EVIDENCES OF CHRISTIANITY, 37½ cents.
———— NATURAL THEOLOGY: edited by Brougham, 90 cents.
PARKER'S (Rev. J.) INVITATIONS TO TRUE HAPPINESS, 37½
cents.
PISE'S (Rev. Dr.) LETTERS TO ADA, 45 cents.
PRIDEAUX'S CONNECTION OF THE OLD AND NEW TESTA
ments, $3 75.
PROTESTANT JESUITISM, by a Protestant, 90 cents.
SANDFORD'S (Rev. P. P.) HELP TO FAITH, 75 cents.
SAURIN'S SERMONS: edited by Bishop Henshaw, $3 75.
SCOTT'S (Rev. J.) LUTHER AND THE REFORMATION, $1 00.
SHOBERL'S HISTORY OF THE PERSECUTIONS OF POPERY,
20 cents.
SHUTTLEWORTH'S CONSISTENCY OF REVELATION, 45 cts
SMEDLEY'S REFORMED RELIGION IN FRANCE, $1 40.

SMITH (Rev. Hugh) ON THE HEART DELINEATED, 45 cents
SMITH AND ANTHON'S STATEMENT OF FACTS, 12½ cents.
STEINMETZ'S NOVITIATE, 50 cents.
STONE'S (Rev. John S.) MYSTERIES OPENED, $1 00
SUFFERINGS (THE) OF CHRIST, by a Layman, $1 00.
SUMMERFIELD'S (Rev. John) SERMONS, $1 75.
TRUE ISSUE SUSTAINED, 12½ cents.
TURNER'S (Rev. S. H.) ESSAY ON THE DISCOURSE AT CA
   PERNAUM, 75 cents.
TURNER'S (S.) SACRED HISTORY OF THE WORLD, $1 25.
UNCLE PHILIP'S EVIDENCES OF CHRISTIANITY, 35 cents
WADDINGTON'S HISTORY OF THE CHURCH, $1 75.
WAINWRIGHT. "NO CHURCH WITHOUT A BISHOP," 25 cts
WHATELEY (Archbishop). CHRISTIANITY INDEPENDENT OF
   THE CIVIL GOVERNMENT, 90 cents.
WHEWELL'S ASTRONOMY AND GENERAL PHYSICS, 50 cts.

Biography.

APOSTLES AND EARLY MARTYRS OF THE CHURCH, 25 cts
BARROW'S (John) LIFE OF PETER THE GREAT, 45 cents.
BANGS'S LIFE OF JAMES ARMINIUS, D.D., 50 cents.
BELKNAP'S (Jeremy) AMERICAN BIOGRAPHY, 3 vols., $1 35.
BELL'S (H. G.) LIFE OF MARY QUEEN OF SCOTS, 85 cents.
BELL'S (Robert) LIFE OF RT. HON. GEORGE CANNING, 50 cts
BONAPARTE (Lucien), MEMOIRS OF, 30 cents.
BONAPARTE (Napoleon), COURT AND CAMP OF, 45 cents.
BOSWELL'S LIFE OF SAMUEL JOHNSON.
BREWSTER'S LIFE OF SIR ISAAC NEWTON, 45 cents.
———————————— LIVES OF GALILEO, TYCHO BRAHE, &c., 45 cts
BURR (Aaron), PRIVATE JOURNAL OF, $4 50.
BUSH'S LIFE OF MOHAMMED, 45 cents.
CALHOUN'S LIFE AND SPEECHES, $1 12½.
———————————— LIFE, 12½ cents.
CAMPBELL'S LIFE OF MRS. SIDDONS, 70 cents.
COBBETT'S LIFE OF GENERAL JACKSON, 40 cents.
COOLEY'S LIFE OF HAYNES: edited by Sprague, 90 cents
CORNWALL'S (Barry) LIFE OF EDMUND KEAN, 65 cents.
COWELL'S LIFE, by Himself. 25 cents.
CROCKETT, SKETCHES OF THE LIFE OF, 50 cents.
CROLY'S LIFE OF GEORGE IV., 45 cents.
CUNNINGHAM'S LIVES OF EMINENT PAINTERS, $2 10.
D'ABRANTES (Duchess), MEMOIRS OF, $1 37½.
DAVIS'S MEMOIRS OF AARON BURR, $3 80.
DISTINGUISHED MEN OF MODERN TIMES (Lives of), 90 cts
DISTINGUISHED FEMALES (Lives of), 35 cents.
DOVER'S (Lord) LIFE OF FREDERIC THE GREAT, 90 cents.
DREW (Samuel), LIFE OF, by his Son, 75 cents.
DWIGHT'S LIVES OF THE SIGNERS OF THE DECLARATION
   OF INDEPENDENCE, 90 cents.
EMINENT INDIVIDUALS, LIVES OF, 3 vols.
FENELON'S LIVES OF ANCIENT PHILOSOPHERS, 45 cents.
FORSTER'S STATESMEN OF THE ENGLISH COMMONWEALTH
FORSYTH'S (Dr.) LIFE OF DR. PROUDFIT, 75 cents.
FRANKLIN (Dr.), LIFE OF, by Himself, 2 vols., 90 cents.

VALUABLE NEW AND STANDARD WORKS

GALT'S (JOHN) LIFE OF LORD BYRON, 40 cents.
GLASS'S LIFE OF WASHINGTON; in Latin, $1 12½.
GODWIN'S LIVES OF THE NECROMANCERS, 65 cents
HEAD'S LIFE OF BRUCE, the African Traveler, 45 cents.
HOGG'S ANECDOTES OF SIR WALTER SCOTT, 60 cents
HOLDICH'S LIFE OF Rev. Dr. WILLBUR FISK, $2 00.
HOLMES'S LIFE OF MOZART, 50 cents.
HORNE'S NEW SPIRIT OF THE AGE, 25 cents
HUNTER'S SACRED BIOGRAPHY, $1 75.
IRVING'S LIFE OF OLIVER GOLDSMITH, 90 cents.
———————— LIFE OF COLUMBUS.
JAMES'S LIFE OF CHARLEMAGNE, 45 cents.
JAMESON'S MEMOIRS OF CELEBRATED FEMALE SOVER
   EIGNS, 80 cents.
JAY'S (JOHN) LIFE, by his SON, $5 00.
JOHNSON'S (Dr.) LIFE, AND SELECT WORKS, 90 cents.
KENDALL'S (AMOS) LIFE OF GENERAL JACKSON.
LEE'S (Mrs.) LIFE OF BARON CUVIER, 50 cents.
LE BAS'S (C. W.) LIFE OF WICLIF, 50 cents.
———————— LIFE OF CRANMER, 2 vols., $1 00.
LIVES OF EMINENT MECHANICS.
LOCKHART'S LIFE OF NAPOLEON, 2 vols., 90 cents.
MACKENZIE'S (A. SLIDELL) LIFE OF PAUL JONES, $1 00.
———————— LIFE OF Com. O. H. PERRY, 90 cts.
MEMES'S MEMOIRS OF THE EMPRESS JOSEPHINE, 45 cents.
M'GUIRE'S OPINIONS AND CHARACTER OF WASHINGTON,
   $1 12½.
MOORE'S (THOMAS) LIFE, LETTERS, &c., OF BYRON, $2 75
———————— LIFE OF LORD EDWARD FITZGERALD, $1 00
NAVIGATORS (EARLY), LIVES OF, 45 cents.
PARK'S (MUNGO) LIFE AND TRAVELS, 45 cents.
PAULDING'S (J. K.) LIFE OF GEORGE WASHINGTON, 90 cts.
PELLICO'S (SILVIO) MEMOIRS AND IMPRISONMENTS, 50 cts
PLUTARCH'S LIVES: translated by LANGHORNE, $2 00.
   The same Work in 4 vols., $3 50.
RENWICK'S LIFE OF DE WITT CLINTON, 45 cents.
———————— LIVES OF JOHN JAY AND ALEXANDER HAMIL
   TON, 45 cents.
ROBERTS'S LIFE AND CORRESPONDENCE OF H. MORE, $1 50
RUSSELL'S LIFE OF OLIVER CROMWELL, 90 cents.
SCOTT'S (Rev. JOHN) LIFE OF LUTHER, $1 00.
SEDGWICK'S (T.) LIFE AND LETTERS OF W. LIVINGSTON
   $2 00.
SOUTHEY'S (ROBERT) LIFE OF LORD NELSON, 45 cents.
SPARKS'S (JARED) WRITINGS OF WASHINGTON, 12 vols., $18 00
———————— AMERICAN BIOGRAPHY, 10 vols., $7 50
   The Volumes sold separately, if desired, 75 cents each.
STEWART'S ADVENTURES IN CAPTURING MURRELL, 90 cts
STILLING'S AUTOBIOGRAPHY, 25 cents.
STONE'S LIFE OF BRANT, THE INDIAN CHIEF, 90 cents.
———————— LIFE OF MATTHIAS THE IMPOSTOR, 62½ cents.
ST. JOHN'S LIVES OF CELEBRATED TRAVELERS, $1 25.
TAYLOR'S (JOHN) "RECORDS OF MY LIFE," $1 50.
TAYLOR'S (W. C.) MODERN BRITISH PLUTARCH, 50 cents.
THATCHER'S BIOGRAPHY OF DISTINGUISHED INDIANS, 90
   cents.

TYLER'S (John) LIFE AND SPEECHES, 50 cents.
——————— HISTORY, CHARACTER, AND POSITION, 12 cents.
WILLIAMS'S LIFE OF ALEXANDER THE GREAT, 45 cents.
WILSON'S LIVES OF ECCENTRIC AND WONDERFUL CHARACTERS, $1 90

History, Ancient and Modern.

ALISON'S HISTORY OF EUROPE FROM 1789 TO 1815, $5 00.
BONNECHOSE'S HISTORY OF THE REFORMERS BEFORE LUTHER, 40 cents.
BUCKE'S RUINS OF ANCIENT CITIES, 90 cents.
BULWER'S (Sir E. L.) ATHENS, ITS RISE AND FALL, $1 20.
BUNNER'S HISTORY OF LOUISIANA TO THE PRESENT TIME 45 cents.
CÆSAR'S COMMENTARIES : translated by WILLIAM DUNCAN, 90 cents.
CRICHTON'S HISTORY OF ARABIA, ANCIENT AND MODERN, 90 cents.
CRICHTON AND WHEATON'S DENMARK, NORWAY, AND SWEDEN, 90 cents.
CROWE'S HISTORY OF FRANCE, 3 vols., $1 75.
DAVIS'S HISTORY OF CHINA, 90 cents.
DUNHAM'S HISTORY OF SPAIN AND PORTUGAL, $2 50.
DUNLAP'S HISTORY OF THE STATE OF NEW YORK, 90 cts.
——————— HISTORY OF THE AMERICAN THEATER, $1 75.
DWIGHT'S HISTORY OF CONNECTICUT, 45 cents.
FERGUSON'S HISTORY OF THE ROMAN REPUBLIC, 45 cents
FLETCHER'S HISTORY OF POLAND, 45 cents.
FLORIAN'S HISTORY OF THE MOORS IN SPAIN, 45 cents.
FRASER'S HISTORY OF MESOPOTAMIA AND ASSYRIA, 45 cts
——————— HISTORICAL AND DESCRIPTIVE ACCOUNT OF PERSIA, 45 cents.
GIBBON'S HISTORY OF ROME, with Notes, by MILMAN, $5 00
GLEIG'S HISTORY OF THE BIBLE, 80 cents.
GOLDSMITH'S HISTORY OF ROME: abridged, 45 cents.
——————— HISTORY OF GREECE : abridged, 45 cents.
GRANT'S HISTORY OF THE NESTORIANS, OR LOST TRIBES, $1 00.
GRATTAN'S HISTORY OF THE NETHERLANDS TO THE REVOLUTION OF 1830, 60 cents.
HALE'S HISTORY OF THE UNITED STATES TO 1817, 2 vols. 90 cents.
HALLAM'S CONSTITUTIONAL HISTORY OF ENGLAND, $2 00.
——————— VIEW OF EUROPE DURING THE MIDDLE AGES. $2 00.
——————— INTRODUCTION TO THE LITERATURE OF EUROPE, $3 75.
HAWKS'S HISTORY OF THE PROT. EPISCOPAL CHURCH IN VIRGINIA, $1 75.
HENRY'S HISTORY OF PHILOSOPHY, 2 vols., 90 cents.
HERODOTUS'S GENERAL HISTORY ; by Rev. W. BELOE, $1 25
HOWITT'S HISTORY OF PRIESTCRAFT IN ALL AGES, 60 cts
ICELAND, GREENLAND, AND THE FAROE ISLANDS, 45 cents

JAMES'S HISTORY of CHIVALRY and the CRUSADES, 44 cts.
JAPAN AND THE JAPANESE, 45 cents.
JARVIS'S CHRONOLOGICAL INTRODUCTION to the HIS
   TORY of the CHURCH, $3 00.
KEIGHTLEY'S HISTORY OF ENGLAND TO 1839, 5 vols., $2 25
LANMAN'S HISTORY OF THE STATE OF MICHIGAN, 13 cents
LIEBER'S GREAT EVENTS.
LIVY'S HISTORY OF ROME: translated by BAKER, 5 vols , $1 25.
LOSSING'S HISTORY OF THE FINE ARTS, 45 cents.
MACKINTOSH'S ENGLAND TO THE 17th CENTURY, $1 50.
MICHELET'S ELEMENTS OF MODERN HISTORY, 45 cents
MILMAN'S HISTORY OF THE JEWS, 3 vols., $1 20.
————— HISTORY OF CHRISTIANITY, $1 90.
MONETTE'S HISTORY of the VALLEY OF THE MISSISSIPPI
MOSHEIM'S ECCLESIASTICAL HISTORY : MACLAINE's Edition.
   $3 50.
   MURDOCK's Edition of the same Work, $7 50.
MULLER'S (Baron VON) HISTORY OF THE WORLD
MURRAY'S HISTORICAL ACCOUNT OF BRITISH AMERICA
   90 cents.
————— HISTORICAL ACCOUNT of BRITISH INDIA, $1 35
NEAL'S HISTORY OF THE PURITANS, $3 50.
PICTORIAL HISTORY OF ENGLAND TO THE REIGN OF
   GEORGE III., profusely Illustrated.
PRESCOTT'S HISTORY OF THE CONQUEST OF MEXICO, 3
   vols., $6 00.
————— HISTORY OF FERDINAND AND ISABELLA, 3
vols., $6 00.
PRIDEAUX'S CONNECTION OF THE OLD AND NEW TESTA
MENTS, $3 75.
ROBERTSON'S HISTORICAL WORKS, 3 vols., 8vo, Maps, $5 00.
————— HISTORY OF THE REIGN OF CHARLES V.,
   $1 75. Abridged, 45 cents.
————— HISTORY OF AMERICA, $1 75. Abridged, 45 cts.
————— HISTORY OF SCOTLAND AND ANCIENT IN-
DIA, $1 75.
ROBINS'S (Mrs.) TALES FROM AMERICAN HISTORY, $1 00.
ROLLIN'S ANCIENT HISTORY, WITH A LIFE OF THE AU-
THOR, $3 75.
RUSSELL and JONES'S HISTORY of MODERN EUROPE, $5 00.
RUSSELL'S (MICHAEL) HISTORY OF EGYPT, 45 cents.
————— HISTORY OF NUBIA AND ABYSSINIA
   45 cents.
————— HISTORY OF THE BARBARY STATES,
   45 cents.
————— HISTORY OF POLYNESIA, 45 cents.
————— HISTORY OF PALESTINE, 45 cents.
SALE'S (Lady) JOURNAL OF DISASTERS IN AFGHANISTAN
12½ cents.
SALLUST'S HISTORY : translated by ROSE, 40 cents.
SCHILLER'S HISTORY OF THE THIRTY YEARS' WAR.
SCOTT'S (Sir W.) HISTORY OF SCOTLAND, $1 20.
————— HISTORY OF DEMONOLOGY, 40 cents
SCOTT'S (Rev. JOHN) LUTHERAN REFORMATION, $1 00.
SEGUR'S HISTORY OF NAPOLEON'S RUSSIAN CAMPAIGN, 90
   cents

SFORZOSI'S HISTORY OF ITALY, 45 cents.
SILK, COTTON, LINEN, WOOL, (HISTORY OF), $3 00.
SISMONDI'S HISTORY OF THE ITALIAN REPUBLICS, 60 cts
SMEDLEY'S HISTORY OF THE REFORMATION IN FRANCE, $1 40.
——————— SKETCHES FROM VENETIAN HISTORY, 90 cents
SMITH'S (H.) HISTORY OF FESTIVALS, GAMES, &c , 45 cents
SMITH'S (H. J.) HISTORY OF EDUCATION, 45 cents.
SPALDING'S HISTORY OF ITALY AND THE ITALIAN ISLANDS $1 35
STONE'S BORDER WARS OF THE AMERICAN REVOLUTION 90 cents.
SWITZERLAND, HISTORY OF, 60 cents.
TAYLOR'S HISTORY OF IRELAND. 90 cents.
THATCHER'S HISTORY OF THE BOSTON TEA-PARTY, 62½ cts.
——————— TALES OF THE AMERICAN REVOLUTION, 35 cents.
THIRLWALL'S HISTORY OF GREECE, 2 vols., $3 50.
THUCYDIDES' GENERAL HISTORY : translated by SMITH, 90 cts
TURNER'S SACRED HISTORY OF THE WORLD, $1 35.
TYTLER'S UNIVERSAL HISTORY, 6 vols., $2 70.
UNCLE PHILIP'S HISTORY OF VIRGINIA, 35 cents.
——————— HISTORY OF NEW YORK, 2 vols., 70 cents.
——————— HISTORY OF LOST GREENLAND, 35 cents
——————— HISTORY OF NEW HAMPSHIRE, 70 cents.
——————— HISTORY OF MASSACHUSETTS, 70 cents
WADDINGTON'S HISTORY OF THE CHURCH, $1 75.
XENOPHON'S HISTORY : translated by SPELMAN, 85 cents

College & School Books.

ABERCROMBIE'S ESSAY ON THE INTELLECTUAL POWERS, 45 cents.
——————— PHILOSOPHY OF THE MORAL FEELINGS, 40 cents.
ALISON'S ESSAYS ON THE NATURE AND PRINCIPLES OF TASTE, 75 cents.
ANTHON'S (CHARLES) LATIN LESSONS, 90 cents.
——————— LATIN PROSE COMPOSITION, 90 cents.
——————— LATIN PROSODY AND METRE, 90 cents
——————— LATIN VERSIFICATION, 90 cents.
——————— KEY TO LATIN VERSIFICATION, 50 cts
——————— ZUMPT'S LATIN GRAMMAR, 90 cents.
——————— COMMENTARIES OF CÆSAR, $1 40
——————— ÆNEID OF VIRGIL. English Notes, $2 00
——————— ECLOGUES AND GEORGICS OF VIRGIL $1 50.
——————— CICERO'S SELECT ORATIONS, $1 20.
——————— SALLUST. With English Notes, 87½ cents
——————— HORACE. With English Notes, $1 75
——————— FIRST GREEK LESSONS. 90 cents.
——————— GREEK PROSE COMPOSITION, 90 cents
——————— GREEK PROSODY AND METRE, 90 cts
——————— GREEK GRAMMAR. 90 cents.
——————— NEW GREEK GRAMMAR, 90 cents.

ANTHON'S (CHARLES) HOMER.   With English Notes, $1 50.
————————————— GREEK READER, FROM THE GERMAN
    OF JACOBS, $1 75.
————————————— ANABASIS OF XENOPHON.
————————————— CLASSICAL DICTIONARY, $4 75.
————————————— SMITH'S DICTIONARY OF GREEK AND
   ROMAN ANTIQUITIES, $4 75.
   The same work, abridged, $1 25
BENNETT'S SYSTEM OF BOOK-KEEPING, $1 50.
BOUCHARLAT'S ELEMENTARY TREATISE ON MECHANICS,
  $2 25.
BOYD'S ELEMENTS OF RHETORIC, 50 cents.
BURKE'S ESSAY ON THE SUBLIME AND BEAUTIFUL, 75 cts
CAMPBELL'S PHILOSOPHY OF RHETORIC, $1 25.
CLARK'S ELEMENTS OF ALGEBRA, $1 00.
DRAPER'S TEXT-BOOK ON CHEMISTRY, $1 75.
EDWARDS'S BOOK-KEEPER'S ATLAS, $2 00.
GLASS'S LIFE OF WASHINGTON, $1 12½.
GRISCOM'S ANIMAL MECHANISM AND PHYSIOLOGY, 45 cts.
HACKLEY'S TREATISE ON ALGEBRA
HAZEN'S PROFESSIONS AND TRADES.   81 Engravings.   75 cts
HEMPEL'S GRAMMAR OF THE GERMAN LANGUAGE, $1 75
HENRY'S HISTORY OF PHILOSOPHY, 90 cents.
KANE'S ELEMENTS OF CHEMISTRY, $2 00.
LEE'S ELEMENTS OF GEOLOGY, 50 cents.
LEWIS'S PLATONIC THEOLOGY, &c., $1 50.
LIDDELL AND SCOTT'S NEW GREEK AND ENGLISH LEX
  ICON, $5 00.
LOOMIS'S TREATISE ON ALGEBRA, $1 25.
MAURY'S PRINCIPLES OF ELOQUENCE, 45 cents.
M'CLINTOCK AND CROOKS'S FIRST BOOK IN LATIN, 75 cts
MILL'S LOGIC, RATIOCINATIVE AND INDUCTIVE, $2 00.
MORSE'S NEW SYSTEM OF GEOGRAPHY, 50 cents.
————————— CEROGRAPHIC MAPS.
NOEL AND CHAPSAL'S NEW SYSTEM OF FRENCH GRAM-
  MAR, 75 cents.
PARKER'S AIDS TO ENGLISH COMPOSITION, 90 cents.
POTTER'S POLITICAL ECONOMY, ITS USES, &c., 50 cents.
PROUDFIT'S PLAUTUS, "THE CAPTIVES."   English Notes, 37½
  cents.
RENWICK'S PRACTICAL MECHANICS, 90 cents.
————————— ELEMENTS OF CHEMISTRY, 75 cents.
————————— FIRST PRINCIPLES OF NATURAL PHILOSOPHY
  75 cents.
SALKELD'S CLASSICAL ANTIQUITIES.
SCHMUCKER'S PSYCHOLOGY, $1 00.
UPHAM'S TREATISE ON THE WILL, $1 25.
————————— ELEMENTS OF MENTAL PHILOSOPHY   2 v.—
  $2 50.   Abridged, $1 25.

Essayists, Belles-Lettres, &c.

ADDISON'S COMPLETE WORKS, 3 vols., $5 50.
————————, SELECTIONS FROM THE SPECTATOR, 90 cents
BACON AND LOCKE'S ESSAYS, 45 cents

BROUGHAM'S PLEASURES AND ADVANTAGES OF SCIENCE, 45 cents.
BUCKE'S BEAUTIES AND SUBLIMITIES OF NATURE, 45 cents
BURKE'S COMPLETE WORKS, 3 vols., $5 00.
————— ESSAY ON THE SUBLIME AND BEAUTIFUL, 75 cts
CHESTERFIELD'S LETTERS TO HIS SON, AND OTHER WRITINGS, $1 75.
CICERO'S OFFICES, ORATIONS, AND CATO AND LÆLIUS, $1 25.
COLERIDGE'S LETTERS, CONVERSATIONS, AND RECOLLECTIONS, 65 cents.
—————, SPECIMENS OF THE TABLE-TALK OF, 70 cents
COMBE'S PHYSIOLOGY APPLIED TO HEALTH AND MENTAL EDUCATION, 45 cents.
DICK ON THE IMPROVEMENT OF SOCIETY BY THE DIFFUSION OF KNOWLEDGE, 45 cents.
D'ISRAELI'S AMENITIES OF LITERATURE.
DEMOSTHENES' ORATIONS; translated by LELAND, 85 cents
DRYDEN'S COMPLETE WORKS, 2 vols., $3 75.
DUTY (THE) OF AMERICAN WOMEN TO THEIR COUNTRY 37½ cents.
EDGEWORTH'S TREATISE ON PRACTICAL EDUCATION, 85 cents.
EVERETT ON PRACTICAL EDUCATION.
FAMILY INSTRUCTOR; OR, DUTIES OF DOMESTIC LIFE, 45 cents.
GRAVES'S (Mrs. A. J.) WOMAN IN AMERICA, 45 cents
HORNE'S NEW SPIRIT OF THE AGE. 25 cents.
HUTTON'S BOOK OF NATURE.
JOHNSON'S (S.) COMPLETE WORKS, 2 vols.
JOHNSON'S (A. B.) TREATISE ON LANGUAGE, $1 75
————— LECTURES TO YOUNG MEN, 45 cents.
LAMB'S ESSAYS OF ELIA, LETTERS, POEMS, &c., $2 00
MACKENZIE'S (HENRY) COMPLETE WORKS, $1 25.
MARTINEAU. HOW TO OBSERVE, 42½ cents.
MATHEWS'S (CORNELIUS) MISCELLANEOUS WRITINGS, $1 00.
MAURY'S PRINCIPLES OF ELOQUENCE, 45 cents.
MONTGOMERY'S LECTURES ON POETRY AND LITERATURE, 45 cents.
MORE'S (HANNAH) COMPLETE WORKS, 7 vols., $6 50. 2 vols., $2 75.
MUDIE'S GUIDE TO THE OBSERVATION OF NATURE, 45 cts
NEELE'S (HENRY) LITERARY REMAINS, $1 00.
NOTT'S COUNSELS TO YOUNG MEN, 50 cents.
POTTER AND EMERSON'S SCHOOL AND THE SCHOOLMASTER, $1 00.
PRESCOTT'S BIOGRAPHICAL AND CRITICAL MISCELLANIES, $2 00.
PURSUIT OF KNOWLEDGE UNDER DIFFICULTIES, 90 cents
SANDS'S (ROBERT C.) WRITINGS, 2 vols., $3 75.
SEDGWICK'S (Miss) MEANS AND ENDS, 45 cents.
SIGOURNEY'S (Mrs. L. H.) LETTERS TO MOTHERS, 90 cents.
————— LETTERS TO YOUNG LADIES, 90 cents.
SMITH'S (H. J.) PLAN OF INSTRUCTION AND HISTORY OF EDUCATION, 45 cents

SOUTHEY (Robert). THE DOCTOR, &c., 45 cents.
VERPLANCK'S DISCOURSES ON AMERICAN HISTORY, 60 cts
———————————— INFLUENCE OF LIBERAL STUDIES, 25 cents.
———————————— INFLUENCE OF MORAL CAUSES, 15 cents.
WIRT'S LETTERS OF THE BRITISH SPY, 60 cents.

Mental and Moral Science, &c.

ABERCROMBIE'S PHILOSOPHY OF THE MORAL FEELINGS
    40 cents.
———————————— ON THE INTELLECTUAL POWERS, 45 cents
ALISON ON THE NATURE AND PRINCIPLES OF TASTE, 75 cts
BACON AND LOCKE'S ESSAYS, AND CONDUCT OF THE UN
    DERSTANDING, 45 cents.
BOYD'S ELEMENTS OF RHETORIC AND LITERARY CRIT'
    CISM, 50 cents.
BURKE'S ESSAY ON THE SUBLIME AND BEAUTIFUL, 75 cts
CAMPBELL'S (George) PHILOSOPHY OF RHETORIC, $1 25
COMBE'S CONSTITUTION OF MAN, 45 cents.
DENDY'S PHILOSOPHY OF MYSTERY, 45 cents.
DYMOND'S PRINCIPLES OF MORALITY: edited by G. Buss.
    $1 37½.
HENRY'S EPITOME OF THE HISTORY OF PHILOSOPHY, 90
    cents.
MARTINEAU'S LETTERS ON MESMERISM, 6½ cents.
MAURY'S PRINCIPLES OF ELOQUENCE, 45 cents.
MILL'S SYSTEM OF LOGIC, RATIOCINATIVE AND INDUC
    TIVE, $2 00.
PARKER'S AIDS TO ENGLISH COMPOSITION, 90 cents.
SAUSSURE'S (Madame de) FIRESIDE FRIEND.
SCHMUCKER'S PSYCHOLOGY, OR MENTAL PHILOSOPHY,
    $1 00.
SEERESS (the) OF PREVORST, 25 cents.
TOWNSHEND'S FACTS IN MESMERISM. With Plates, 75 cents
UNCLE SAM'S RECOMMENDATIONS OF PHRENOLOGY, 45 cts.
UPHAM'S IMPERFECT AND DISORDERED MENTAL ACTION,
    45 cents.
———————————— ELEMENTS OF MENTAL PHILOSOPHY, $2 50.
    Abridged, $1 25.
———————————— PHILOSOPHICAL AND PRACTICAL TREATISE ON
    THE WILL, $1 25.

Natural Science &c.

BELL'S MECHANISM OF THE HAND, 60 cents.
BIGELOW (Jacob) ON THE USEFUL ARTS.
BIRDS, NATURAL HISTORY OF, 45 cents.
BOUCHARLAT'S ELEMENTARY TREATISE ON MECHANICS
    $2 25.
BRANDE'S ENCYCLOPEDIA OF SCIENCE AND ART, $4 00
BREWSTER'S LETTERS ON NATURAL MAGIC, 45 cents.
BROWNE'S TREES OF AMERICA, $5 00.
CHAPTAL'S CHEMISTRY APPLIED TO AGRICULTURE, 45 cts
COMBE'S PRINCIPLES OF PHYSIOLOGY, 45 cents

DANIELL'S ILLUSTRATIONS OF NATURAL PHILOSOPHY
  68¼ cents.
DICK'S CELESTIAL SCENERY, 45 cents.
————— SIDEREAL HEAVENS, 45 cents.
————— PRACTICAL ASTRONOMER, 50 cents.
DRAPER'S CHEMICAL ORGANIZATION OF PLANTS, $2 50
————— TEXT-BOOK OF CHEMISTRY, 75 cents.
DYEING, CALICO-PRINTING, &c., $3 50.
ELEPHANT, NATURAL HISTORY OF THE, 45 cents.
EULER'S LETTERS ON NATURAL PHILOSOPHY, edited by
  BREWSTER and GRISCOM, 45 cents
GRISCOM'S ANIMAL MECHANISM AND PHYSIOLOGY, 45 cts
HASWELL'S ENGINEERS' AND MECHANICS' POCKET-BOOK,
  $1 25.
HERSCHEL (J. F. W.) ON THE STUDY OF NATURAL PHILOS-
  OPHY, 60 cents.
HIGGINS'S PHYSICAL CONDITION AND PHENOMENA OF THE
  EARTH, 45 cents.
HUMBOLDT'S COSMOS; A SURVEY OF THE PHYSICAL HIS-
  TORY OF THE UNIVERSE.
INSECTS, NATURAL HISTORY OF, 90 cents.
KANE'S ELEMENTS OF CHEMISTRY : edited by DRAPER, $2 00.
LEE'S ELEMENTS OF GEOLOGY FOR POPULAR USE, 50 cts.
MUDIE'S GUIDE TO THE OBSERVATION OF NATURE, 45 cts.
MOSELEY'S ILLUSTRATIONS OF MECHANICS, 45 cents.
OLMSTEAD'S LETTERS ON ASTRONOMY.
POTTER'S SCIENCE APPLIED TO THE DOMESTIC ARTS, &c
QUADRUPEDS, NATURAL HISTORY OF, 45 cents.
RENWICK'S PRACTICAL MECHANICS, 90 cents.
————— FIRST PRINCIPLES OF CHEMISTRY, 75 cents.
————— FIRST PRINCIPLES OF NATURAL PHILOSOPHY
  75 cents.
SACRED PHILOSOPHY OF THE SEASONS.
SOMERVILLE'S (MARY) CONNECTION OF THE PHYSICAL
  SCIENCES, 50 cents.
UNCLE PHILIP'S AMERICAN FOREST, 35 cents.
————— NATURAL HISTORY, 35 cents.
VEGETABLE SUBSTANCES USED FOR THE FOOD OF MAN,
  45 cents.
WHEWELL'S ASTRONOMY AND GENERAL PHYSICS, 50 cts
WHITE'S NATURAL HISTORY OF SELBORNE, 45 cents
WYATT'S MANUAL OF CONCHOLOGY, $2 75.   Colored Plates.
  $7 50.

Voyages and Travels.

ALTOWAN; OR, INCIDENTS OF LIFE IN THE ROCKY MOUNTAINS,
  $1 25.
ANTHON'S (C E.) PILGRIMAGE TO TREVES, 75 cents.
BARROW'S VOYAGES WITHIN THE ARCTIC REGIONS, 50 cts.
————— PITCAIRN'S ISLAND AND MUTINY OF THE SHIP
  BOUNTY, 45 cents.
BROWNE'S ETCHINGS OF A WHALING CRUISE, $2 00
BUCKINGHAM'S TRAVELS IN AMERICA.   Engravings, $3 50
CHANGE FOR THE AMERICAN NOTES, 12½ cents

CIRCUMNAVIGATION OF THE GLOBE, 45 cents.
COKE'S TRAVELS IN THE UNITED STATES, NOVA SCOTIA
    AND CANADA, 75 cents.
COLTON'S FOUR YEARS IN GREAT BRITAIN, 90 cents.
COOK'S VOYAGES ROUND THE WORLD.   With a Sketch of his
    Life, 37½ cents.
DANA'S TWO YEARS BEFORE THE MAST, 45 cents.
DARWIN'S VOYAGE OF A NATURALIST, $1 00.
DAVENPORT'S PERILOUS ADVENTURES, 45 cents.
DE KAY'S SKETCHES OF TURKEY, $2 00.
DICKENS'S AMERICAN NOTES FOR GENERAL CIRCULA
    TION, 12½ cents.
DRAKE, CAVENDISH, AND DAMPIER, LIVES AND VOYAGES
    OF, 45 cents.
DURBIN'S OBSERVATIONS IN EUROPE, 2 vols., $2 00
————— TRAVELS IN THE EAST, 2 vols., $2 00.
ELLIS'S POLYNESIAN RESEARCHES, 4 vols., $2 50.
EMERSON'S LETTERS FROM THE ÆGEAN, 75 cents.
FARNHAM'S (Mrs. ELIZA W.) LIFE IN PRAIRIE LAND, 50 cents.
FEATHERSTONHAUGH'S EXCURSIONS THROUGH THE SLAVE
    STATES, &c., 25 cents.
FIDLER'S OBSERVATIONS ON PROFESSIONS, &c., IN THE
    UNITED STATES AND CANADA, 60 cents.
FISK'S TRAVELS IN EUROPE, $3 25.
FLAGG'S TRAVELS IN THE FAR WEST, $1 50.
GRANT'S NESTORIANS; OR, THE LOST TRIBES, $1 00.
GREEN'S TEXIAN EXPEDITION AGAINST MIER.   Plates, $2 00
HAIGHT'S (Mrs.) LETTERS FROM THE OLD WORLD, $1 75.
HEAD'S (Sir GEORGE) MANUFACTURING DISTRICTS OF ENG
    LAND, $1 12½.
HEAD'S (Sir FRANCIS B.) LIFE AND ADVENTURES OF BRUCE,
    THE AFRICAN TRAVELER, 45 cents.
HOFFMAN'S WINTER IN THE WEST, $1 50.
HUMBOLDT'S TRAVELS AND RESEARCHES, 45 cents.
HUMPHREY'S GREAT BRITAIN, FRANCE, AND BELGIUM,
    $1 75.
INGRAHAM'S SOUTHWEST, $1 50.
JACOBS'S SCENES, INCIDENTS, AND ADVENTURES IN THE
    PACIFIC OCEAN, $1 25.
JAMESON'S DISCOVERIES AND ADVENTURES IN AFRICA, 45
    cents.
JAMESON'S (Mrs.) VISITS AND SKETCHES AT HOME AND
    ABROAD, $1 00.
KAY'S TRAVELS AND RESEARCHES IN CAFFRARIA, 85 cents
KENDALL'S TEXAN SANTA FE EXPEDITION, $2 50.
KEPPEL'S EXPEDITION TO BORNEO, 50 cents.
KOHL'S SKETCHES IN IRELAND, 12½ cents.
LANDERS' (R. and J.) JOURNAL OF TRAVEL IN AFRICA, 90 cts.
LATROBE'S RAMBLER IN MEXICO, 65 cents.
————— RAMBLER IN NORTH AMERICA, $1 10.
LESLIE, &c., DISCOVERIES AND ADVENTURES IN THE POLAR
    SEAS, 45 cents.
LESTER'S GLORY AND SHAME OF ENGLAND, $1 50
LEWIS AND CLARK'S TRAVELS BEYOND THE ROCKY
    MOUNTAINS, 90 cents.
MACKENZIE'S YEAR IN SPAIN, $2 25

MACKENZIE'S SPAIN REVISITED, $1 75.
———————— AMERICAN IN ENGLAND, $1 50
MARRYAT'S TRAVELS OF MONSIEUR VIOLET IN CALIFOR
    NIA, 12½ cents.
MILLER'S CONDITION OF GREECE, 37½ cents.
MORGAN'S (Lady) FRANCE, 70 cents.
MORRELL'S (Captain) FOUR VOYAGES TO THE SOUTH SEA
    $1 50.
MORRELL'S (Mrs. A. J.) VOYAGE TO THE SOUTH SEA, 62½ cts
MOTT'S TRAVELS IN EUROPE AND THE EAST, $1 00
NEW ORLEANS AS I FOUND IT, 25 cents.
OLIN'S TRAVELS IN THE HOLY LAND, $2 50.
OWEN'S VOYAGES TO EASTERN AFRICA, $1 12½.
PARK'S TRAVELS IN AFRICA, 45 cents.
PARROT'S JOURNEY TO MOUNT ARARAT, 50 cents.
PARRY'S VOYAGES TOWARD THE NORTH POLE, 90 cents.
PERILS OF THE SEA, 35 cents.
PHELPS'S (Mrs.) CAROLINE WESTERLEY, 35 cents.
POLO'S (Marco) TRAVELS, 45 cents.
PORTER'S CONSTANTINOPLE AND ITS ENVIRONS, $1 50.
PUCKLER MUSKAU. TUTTI FRUTTI, 50 cents.
PYM'S (Arthur Gordon) NARRATIVE, 65 cents.
REED AND MATHESON'S VISIT to the AMERICAN CHURCH-
    ES, $1 30.
REYNOLDS'S VOYAGE OF THE U. S. FRIGATE POTOMAC
            Round the World, $3 25.
———————— LETTERS ON THE EXPLORING EXPEDITION,
            $1 50.
ROBERTS'S EMBASSY TO THE COURTS OF SIAM, COCHIN-
    China, &c., $1 75.
SALE'S (Lady) JOURNAL OF DISASTERS IN AFGHANISTAN,
    12½ cents.
SARGENT'S AMERICAN ADVENTURE BY LAND AND SEA,
    90 cents.
SCHROEDER'S SHORES OF THE MEDITERRANEAN, $1 75.
SEAWARD'S NARRATIVE OF HIS SHIPWRECK, 37½ cents.
SEDGWICK'S (Miss) LETTERS FROM ABROAD TO KINDRED
    at Home, $1 00.
SIEBOLD'S MANNERS AND CUSTOMS OF THE JAPANESE,
    45 cents.
STEPHENS'S INCIDENTS of TRAVEL in CENTRAL AMERICA.
            Map and 88 Engravings, $5 00.
———————— INCIDENTS OF TRAVEL IN YUCATAN.   120 En
            gravings, $5 00.
———————— INCIDENTS OF TRAVEL IN GREECE, TURKEY,
            Russia, and Poland.   Engravings, $1 75.
———————— INCIDENTS OF TRAVEL IN EGYPT, ARABIA
            Petræa, and the Holy Land.   Engravings, $1 75.
ST JOHN'S LIVES OF CELEBRATED TRAVELERS, $1 25.
TASISTRO'S TRAVELS IN THE SOUTHERN STATES, $1 50.
THINGS AS THEY ARE IN THE MIDDLE AND SOUTHERN
    States, 75 cents.
TROLLOPE'S PARIS AND THE PARISIANS IN 1835, $1 50.
TYTLER'S DISCOVERIES ON THE NORTHERN COASTS OF
    America, 45 cents.
UNCLE PHILIP'S WHALE FISHERY AND POLAR SEAS, 70 cts

VOYAGES ROUND THE WORLD SINCE THE DEATH OF CAP
  TAIN COOK, 45 cents.
WOLFF'S MISSION TO BOKHARA. Engravings, $2 00.
WRANGELL'S EXPEDITION TO SIBERIA, POLAR SEA, &c
  45 cents.

Splendidly Embellished Works.

AIKIN (Dr.) AND BARBAULD'S (Mrs.) EVENINGS AT HOME,
  $1 20.
BEATTIE (JAMES) AND COLLINS'S (W.) POETICAL WORKS
BIBLE, HARPER'S ILLUMINATED, $22 50.
BOOK OF COMMON PRAYER. $6 00.
BUNYAN'S PILGRIM'S PROGRESS, 75 cents.
BYRON'S CHILDE HAROLD, $5 00.
COWPER'S (WILLIAM) POEMS.
DEFOE'S ROBINSON CRUSOE, $1 25.
ENGLAND, PICTORIAL HISTORY OF.
FAIRY BOOK, ILLUSTRATED, 75 cents.
GOLDSMITH'S (OLIVER) POETICAL WORKS
HIEROGLYPHICAL BIBLE, 70 cents.
LIFE OF CHRIST, in the Words of the Evangelists, $1 00
MILTON'S POETICAL WORKS.
SHAKSPEARE, HARPER'S ILLUMINATED, $5 00.
SUE'S WANDERING JEW, ILLUSTRATED, $5 00
THOMSON'S SEASONS.

Medical and Surgical Science, &c.

BAYLE'S ELEMENTARY TREATISE ON ANATOMY, 87½ cents
CHAILLY'S PRACTICAL TREATISE ON MIDWIFERY, $2 00
COOPER'S DICTIONARY OF PRACTICAL SURGERY, $3 87½.
COPLAND'S DICTIONARY OF PRACTICAL MEDICINE, 3 vols.,
  vols. 1 and 2 now ready, $5 00 per volume.
CRUVEILHIER'S ANATOMY OF THE HUMAN BODY, $3 00.
DOANE'S SURGERY ILLUSTRATED. 25 Plates, $4 50.
FERRIS'S TREATISE ON EPIDEMIC CHOLERA, $1 25.
GALT'S TREATMENT OF INSANITY.
GOOD'S STUDY OF MEDICINE. $5 00.
GOVE'S (MARY S.) LECTURES TO WOMEN ON ANATOMY AND
  PHYSIOLOGY, 75 cents.
GUY'S PRINCIPLES OF MEDICAL JURISPRUDENCE, $3 00
HOOPER'S MEDICAL DICTIONARY, $3 00
JOHNSON'S ECONOMY OF HEALTH, 65 cents.
KITCHINER'S DIRECTIONS FOR INVIGORATING AND PRO-
  LONGING LIFE, 40 cents.
MAGENDIE'S TREATISE ON HUMAN PHYSIOLOGY, $2 00.
MASSE'S POCKET ANATOMICAL ATLAS, 442 Figures, engraved
  on Steel, and beautifully colored. $7 50 ; with Plates uncolored, $3 00
NELIGAN ON MEDICINES, THEIR USES ETC, $1 75.
PAINE'S INSTITUTES OR PHILOSOPHY OF MEDICINE
PARIS'S PHARMACOLOGIA, $1 50.
REESE'S TREATISE ON EPIDEMIC CHOLERA, 75 cents

REVERE'S PRACTICAL MEDICINE.
SMITH ON EPIDEMICS, $1 00.
SPURZHEIM'S PHRENOLOGY.
STEWART ON THE DISEASES OF CHILDREN, $1 50.
TICKNOR'S PHILOSOPHY OF LIVING, 45 cents.

Dictionaries and Encyclopedias.

ANTHON'S CLASSICAL DICTIONARY, $4 75.
———————— DICTIONARY OF GREEK AND ROMAN ANTIQUI-
   TIES, $4 75.
———————— DICTIONARY OF ANTIQUITIES, ABRIDGED, $1 25
BRANDE'S ENCYCLOPEDIA OF SCIENCE AND ART, $4 00.
BROWN'S DICTIONARY OF THE HOLY BIBLE, $1 75.
COBB'S MINIATURE LEXICON OF THE ENGLISH LANGUAGE,
   50 cents.
COOPER'S DICTIONARY OF PRACTICAL SURGERY, $3 87½.
COPLAND'S DICTIONARY OF PRACTICAL MEDICINE, 3 vols.,
   vols. 1 and 2 now ready, $5 00 per volume.
CRABB'S ENGLISH SYNONYMS EXPLAINED, $2 37½.
GARDNER'S FARMER'S DICTIONARY, $1 50.
HOOPER'S MEDICAL DICTIONARY, $3 00.
LIDDELL AND SCOTT'S NEW GREEK AND ENGLISH LEX-
   ICON, $5 00.
M'CULLOCH'S UNIVERSAL GAZETTEER, $6 50.
WEBSTER'S (N.) DICTIONARY OF THE ENGLISH LANGUAGE,
   $3 50.
WEBSTER (Thomas) AND PARKES'S (Mrs.) ENCYCLOPEDIA OF
   DOMESTIC ECONOMY, $3 75.

Politics, Political Economy, &c.

BULWER'S (E. L.) ENGLAND AND THE ENGLISH, 85 cents.
BULWER'S (H. L.) FRANCE, 90 cents.
CALHOUN'S LIFE, AND SELECTIONS FROM HIS SPEECHES
   $1 00.
———————— LIFE, 12½ cents.
CAMP'S DEMOCRACY, 45 cents.
DEFENSE OF THE WHIGS, 25 cents.
DOWNING'S (Major Jack) LETTERS TO MR. DWIGHT, 62½ cts
DUER'S CONSTITUTIONAL JURISPRUDENCE, 45 cents.
LESTER'S GLORY AND SHAME OF ENGLAND, $1 50.
LIEBER'S ESSAYS ON PROPERTY AND LABOR, 45 cents.
M'CULLOCH'S UNIVERSAL GAZETTEER, $6 50.
PAULDING'S VIEW OF SLAVERY IN THE UNITED STATES,
   62½ cents.
POTTER'S POLITICAL ECONOMY, 50 cents.
SEDGWICK'S (Theo.) PUBLIC AND PRIVATE ECONOMY, $1 80
STORY ON THE CONSTITUTION.
TYLER'S LIFE AND SPEECHES, 50 cents.
WAKEFIELD'S ENGLAND AND AMERICA, $1 25.
WIRT'S LETTERS OF THE BRITISH SPY, 60 cents

Poetry and the Drama.

ÆSCHYLUS'S TRAGEDIES, 45 cents.
BROOKS'S RIVALS OF ESTE, 50 cents.
BRYANT'S SELECTIONS FROM AMERICAN POETS, 45 cents
BULWER'S SIAMESE TWINS, 45 cents.
——————— LADY OF LYONS, 40 cents.
——————— SEA CAPTAIN, 20 cents.
——————— LIFE AND POEMS OF SCHILLER, 90 cents.
——————— REBEL, and other Tales, 50 cents.
——————— RICHELIEU, 45 cents.
EURIPIDES' TRAGEDIES, $1 30.
FORD'S DRAMATIC WORKS, 85 cents.
GOLDSMITH'S (Oliver) POETICAL WORKS.
HALLECK'S ALNWICK CASTLE, and other Poems, $1 12½.
——————— FANNY, with other Poems, $1 12½.
——————— SELECTIONS FROM BRITISH POETS, 90 cents
HOFFMAN'S POEMS, COMPLETE, 50 cents.
HOMER'S ILIAD AND ODYSSEY, $1 35.
HORACE AND PHÆDRUS, 87½ cents.
JAMES'S BLANCHE OF NAVARRE, 25 cents.
JUVENAL AND PERSIUS'S SATIRES, 45 cents.
LONGFELLOW'S POEMS, COMPLETE, 50 cents.
MASSINGER'S DRAMATIC WORKS, $1 30.
MILTON'S POETICAL WORKS.
MORGAN'S (Lady) DRAMATIC SCENES FROM REAL LIFE, 66
   cents.
OVID'S METAMORPHOSES AND EPISTLES, 87½ cents.
PELAYO; OR, THE CAVERN OF COVADONGA, 62½ cents.
PINDAR AND ANACREON'S ODES, 45 cents.
SCOTT'S DOOM OF DEVORGOIL, 35 cents.
SHAKSPEARE'S DRAMATIC WORKS, $6 50.
——————— DRAMATIC WORKS AND POEMS, $2 75.
——————————, HARPER'S ILLUMINATED.
SIGOURNEY'S (Mrs.) POCAHONTAS, 90 cents.
SMITH'S POWHATAN, $1 00.
SOPHOCLES'S TRAGEDIES, 45 cents.
THOMAS'S BEECHEN TREE, 50 cents.
THOMSON'S SEASONS.
TYLER'S AHASUERUS, 45 cents.
——————— DEATH; OR, MEDORUS'S DREAM, 45 cents.
VIRGIL'S ECLOGUES, GEORGICS, AND ÆNEID, 90 cents.

Juvenile Works.

AIKIN (Dr.) AND BARBAULD'S (Mrs.) EVENINGS AT HOME,
   $1 20.
BLAKE'S HISTORY OF THE AMERICAN REVOLUTION.
——————— JUVENILE COMPANION.
BOARDING OUT, 37½ cents.
CATE'S (Miss Jane) YEAR WITH THE FRANKLINS, 37½ cents
CLERGYMAN'S (the) ORPHAN, 35 cents.
CONQUEST AND SELF-CONQUEST, 37½ cents.
COUSINS (the), 37½ cents.
DANA'S (Mrs. Mary S. B.) FORECASTLE TOM, 37½ cents

VALUABLE NEW AND STANDARD WORKS

UNCLE PHILIP'S AMERICAN FOREST, 35 cents
———————————— EVIDENCES OF CHRISTIANITY, 35 cents.
———————————— NATURAL HISTORY, 35 cents.
———————————— WHALE FISHERY AND POLAR SEAS, 70 cts
WEALTH AND WORTH, 45 cents.
WHAT'S TO BE DONE ! 45 cents.
WOMAN AN ENIGMA, 37½ cents.

Miscellaneous Works.

BEECHER'S (Miss C. E.) ADDRESS, 12½ cents.
BREMER'S (Miss FREDRIKA) NOVELS, $1 50.
CATE'S (Miss JANE) YEAR WITH THE FRANKLINS, 37½ cents
COMFORTER (THE); OR, CONSOLATIONS FOR MOURNERS,
    45 cents
DAYS OF QUEEN MARY, 25 cents.
DUER'S SPEECH, 12½ cents.
EDGEWORTH'S (Miss) TALES AND NOVELS, 10 vols., 75 cents
    per volume
ELIZABETH BENTON, 37½ cents.
ELLIS'S (Mrs.) TEMPER AND TEMPERAMENT, 37½ cents.
EMBURY'S (EMMA C.) BLIND GIRL, 37½ cents.
FEUERBACH'S REMARKABLE GERMAN CRIMINAL TRIALS,
    50 cents.
GEORGIA SCENES, 90 cents.
GILMAN'S (Mrs. C.) RECOLLECTIONS OF A HOUSEKEEPER,
    45 cents.
———————————— LOVE'S PROGRESS, 65 cents.
———————————— RECOLLECTIONS OF A SOUTHERN MAT-
    RON, 90 cents.
GOLDSMITH'S VICAR OF WAKEFIELD, 35 cents.
GOVE'S (MARY S.) LECTURES TO WOMEN ON ANATOMY AND
    PHYSIOLOGY, 75 cents.
GRAVES'S (Mrs. A. J.) WOMEN IN AMERICA, 45 cents.
HASWELL'S ENGINEERS' AND MECHANICS' POCKET-BOOK,
    $1 25.
HAZEN'S POPULAR TECHNOLOGY, 90 cents.
HOES AND WAY'S ANECDOTICAL OLIO, $1 00.
ISABEL ; OR, THE TRIALS OF THE HEART, 37½ cents.
JAMESON'S (Mrs.) VISITS AND SKETCHES AT HOME AND
    ABROAD, $1 00.
KEEPING HOUSE AND HOUSEKEEPING, 37½ cents.
LLOYD'S (Mrs. M. B.) PARLOR MELODIES, FOR THE PIANO-
    FORTE, $1 00.
MASON'S ZION'S SONGSTER, 25 cents.
MATHEWS'S MISCELLANEOUS WRITINGS, $1 00.
MORSE'S ATLAS OF CEROGRAPHIC MAPS, in Nos., 25 cents
    each.
NOTE-BOOK OF A COUNTRY CLERGYMAN, 37½ cents
ORME'S UNCLE JOHN, 37½ cents.
PAULDING'S JOHN BULL AND BROTHER JONATHAN, 25 cts.
———————————— LETTERS FROM THE SOUTH, $1 25.
PERCY ANECDOTES, $2 00.
PHILOSOPHICAL EMPEROR (THE), 37½ cents.
POTTER'S HAND-BOOK FOR READERS AND STUDENTS, 45
    cents.

————————————

Harper's New Miscellany
Of Popular Sterling Literature.

Now in course of publication, price fifty cents a volume

I., II. Prof. Whewell's Elements of Morality and Polity
III. Dendy's Philosophy of Mystery.
IV. Holmes's Life and Letters of Mozart.
V. Dick's Practical Astronomer.
VI., VII. Mackenzie's Life of Paul Jones.
VIII. Parrot's Ascent of Mount Ararat.
IX. Remarkable German Criminal Trials.
X., XI. Darwin's Voyage of a Naturalist.
XII. Farnham's Life in Prairie Land.
XIII. Barrow's Voyages in the Arctic Regions.
XIV. Somerville on the Physical Sciences.
XV. The Biblical Legends of the Mussulmans.
XVI. Bell's Life of George Canning.
XVII. Taylor's Modern British Plutarch.
XVIII. Keppel's Expedition to Borneo.
XIX. Schiller's History of the Thirty Years' War.

VALUABLE NEW AND STANDARD WORKS

Harper's Family Library.

Each work sold separately, price by the set of 173 volumes, $77 05.

Harper's Family Library continued.

73. Russell's Barbary States.
74. Natural History of Insects. Vol. II.
75, 76. Paulding's Life of Washington.
77. Ticknor's Philosophy of Living.
78. Physical Condition of the Earth.
79. Greene's History of Italy.
80, 81. China and the Chinese. By Davis.
82 Circumnavigation of the Globe.
83. Dick's Celestial Scenery.
84. Sacred History of the World. Vol. III.
85. Griscom's Animal Mechanism.
86–91. Tytler's Universal History: continued by Dr. Nares
92, 93. Life of Franklin, &c.
94, 95. Pursuit of Knowledge under Difficulties.
96, 97. Paley's Natural Theology.
98. Natural History of Birds.
99. Dick's Sidereal Heavens.
100. Upham on Imperfect and Disordered Mental Action.
101, 102. Murray's British America.
103. Lossing on the Fine Arts.
104. Natural History of Quadrupeds.
105. Life and Travels of Mungo Park.
106. Two Years before the Mast.
107, 108. Parry's Three Voyages for the Discovery of a Northwest Pas
sage.
109, 110. Life of Dr. Johnson, with Selections from his Writings
111. Bryant's American Poets.
112, 113. Halleck's British Poets.
114–118. Keightley's History of England.
119, 120. Hale's United States.
121, 122. Irving's Life of Goldsmith, with Selections from his Writings
123, 124. Distinguished Men of Modern Times.
125. Life of De Witt Clinton.
126, 127. Life of Commodore Perry.
128. Life and Travels of Bruce.
129. Lives of John Jay and Alexander Hamilton.
130. Brewster's Lives of Galileo, Tycho Brahe, and Kepler.
131. History of Iceland, Greenland, and the Faroe Islands.
132. Manners and Customs of the Japanese.
133. Dwight's History of Connecticut.
134, 135. Ruins of Ancient Cities.
136, 137. History of Denmark.
138. Camp on Democracy.
139. Lanman's Michigan.
140. Fenelon's Lives of the Ancient Philosophers.
141, 142. Count Segur's History of Napoleon's Expedition to Russia
143, 144. History of Philosophy.
145. Bucke's Beauties, Harmonies, and Sublimities of Nature.
146. Lieber's Essays on Property.
147. White's Natural History of Selborne.
148. Wrangell's Expedition to Siberia.
149, 150. Popular Technology.
151–153. Italy. By Spaulding.
154, 155. Lewis and Clarke's Travels.
156. Smith's History of Education.

Harper's Family Library continued.

157. Mesopotamia and Assyria.
158. Russell's History of Polynesia.
159. Perilous Adventures.
160. Constitutional Jurisprudence of the United States   By Dr. Duer.
161–163. Belknap's American Biography.
164. Natural History of the Elephant.
165. Potter's Hand-book for Readers.
166. Woman in America.
167, 168. Border Wars of the Revolution.   By W. L. Stone.
169 Vegetable Substances used for Food.
170. Michelet's Elements of Modern History : edited by Rev. Dr. Potter.
171. Bacon's Essays, and Locke on the Understanding.
172. Voyages round the World.
173. Travels of Marco Polo.

Harper's Family Classical Library.

Containing 36 vols. 18mo.   Price per set, $15 86.

1, 2. Xenophon.   Translated by Spelman and Cooper
3, 4. Demosthenes.   Translated by Leland.
5. Sallust.   Translated by Rose.
6, 7. Cæsar.   Translated by Duncan.
8–10. Cicero.   Translated by Duncan.
11, 12. Virgil.   Translated by Wrangham, Sotheby, and Dryden.
13. Æschylus.   Translated by Potter.
14. Sophocles.   Translated by Francklin.
15–17. Euripides.   Translated by Potter.
18, 19. Horace and Phædrus.   Translated by Francis, Smart, &c.
20, 21. Ovid.   Translated by Dryden and others.
22, 23. Thucydides.   Translated by Smith.
24–28. Livy.   Translated by Baker.
29–31. Herodotus.   Translated by Beloe.
32–34. Homer.   Translated by Pope.
35. Juvenal.   Translated by Badham : and Persius, by Drummond.
36. Pindar.   Translated by Wheelwright : and Anacreon, by Bourne.

Boys' and Girls' Library.

Containing 32 vols. 18mo.   Sold separately or in sets
Price $10 75 per set.

1. Lives of the Apostles and Early Martyrs.
2, 3. The Swiss Family Robinson ; or, Adventures of a Father and Mother and four Sons on a Desert Island.
4, 13, 18. Sunday Evenings.   Comprising Scripture Stories.   Engr's.
5. The Son of a Genius.   By Mrs. Hofland.
6. Uncle Philip's Natural History ; or, Conversations about Tools and Trades among the Inferior Animals.
7, 8. Indian Traits ; or, Manners, Customs, and Character of the North American Indians.   By Thatcher.

Boys' and Girls' Library continued.

9-11. Tales from American History. By the Author of "American Popular Lessons."
12. The Young Crusoe; or, the Shipwrecked Boy. By Mrs. Hofland.
14. Perils of the Sea, being authentic Narratives of remarkable and affecting Disasters upon the Deep.
15. Sketches of the Lives of Distinguished Females. By an American Lady.
16. Caroline Westerley; or, the Young Traveler from Ohio. By Mrs A. H. L. Phelps.
17. The Clergyman's Orphan; The Infidel Reclaimed; and Jane Clark, the Orphan. By a Clergyman. Engravings.
19. The Ornaments Discovered. By Mrs. Hugh.
20. Uncle Philip's Evidences of Christianity.
21. Uncle Philip's Conversations about the History of Virginia.
22. The American Forest; or, Uncle Philip's Conversations about the Trees of America.
23, 24. Uncle Philip's Conversations with the Children about the History of New York.
25. Tales of the American Revolution. By B. B. Thatcher.
26, 27. Uncle Philip's Account of the Whale Fishery and the Polar Seas.
28. Uncle Philip's Conversations about the History of the Lost Colony of Greenland.
29, 30. Uncle Philip's History of Massachusetts.
31, 32. Uncle Philip's History of New Hampshire.

Harper's School District Library
Of Valuable Standard Literature.

Each volume sold separately, at 37½ cents.

First Series—$20 with the Case, or $19 without the Case

1, 2. Paulding's Life of Washington.
3. Poor Rich Man and Rich Poor Man.
4, 5. The Swiss Family Robinson.
6, 7. Natural History of Insects.
8. The Son of a Genius. By Mrs. Hofland
9-11. Tales from American History.
12. Tales from the American Revolution.
13, 14. Lockhart's Life of Napoleon.
15. Combe's Physiology, &c.
16, 17. Thatcher's Indian Traits, &c.
18. Discovery and Adventure in Africa.
19. Conversations about Trees.
20. Guide to the Observation of Nature.
21. Perils of the Sea.
22. Abercrombie on the Intellectual Powers.
23. Montgomery's Lectures on Poetry.
24. Dick's Celestial Scenery.
25. Russell's History of Palestine.
26. James's History of Chivalry.
27. Brewster's Life of Newton.

VALUABLE NEW AND STANDARD WORKS

School District Library continued.

28. Live and Let Live. By Miss Sedgwick.
29, 30. Davis's China and Chinese.
31. Circumnavigation of the Globe.
32. Life of Alexander the Great.
33, 34. Euler on Natural Philosophy.
35. Barrow's Life of Peter the Great.
36, 37. Russell's Life of Cromwell.
38. Dick on the Improvement of Society
39. Physical Condition of the Earth.
40. Abercrombie on the Moral Feeling
41, 42. Jameson's Female Sovereigns.
43. Uncle Philip's History of Virginia
44. The Ornaments Discovered.
45. Uncle Philip's Natural History.
46, 47. Uncle Philip's Whale Fishery.
48. Lives and Voyages of Drake, Cavendish, and Dampier
49, 50. Dunlap's History of New York.

Second Series—$20 with the Case, or $19 without the Case

51, 52. Life and Works of Franklin.
53, 54. Buel's Farmer's Instructor.
55, 56. Pursuit of Knowledge under Difficulties.
57. Griscom's Animal Mechanism.
58. Natural History of the Elephant.
59. Vegetable Substances used for Food.
60–65. Tytler's Universal History.
66. Moseley's Illustrations of Mechanics.
67. The Polar Seas and Regions.
68, 69. Paley's Natural Theology.
70–79. Sparks's American Biography.
80. Humboldt's Travels.
81. Goldsmith's History of Greece.
82. Natural History of Birds.
83. Renwick's Familiar Illustrations of Natural Philosophy
84, 85. Selections from the Spectator.
86. Lee's Elements of Geology.
87. Goldsmith's Rome. Abridged.
88. Armstrong on Agriculture.
89. Natural History of Quadrupeds.
90. Chaptal's Agricultural Chemistry.
91. Dwight's Lives of the Signers of the Declaration of Independence
92–95. Plutarch's Lives.

Third Series—$20 with the Case, or $19 without the Case.

96, 97. Hale's History of the United States.
98. Brewster's Letters on Natural Magic.
99. Renwick's Applications of Mechanics.
100, 101. Parry's Voyages of Discovery.
102–106. Keightley's History of England.
107, 108. Mackenzie's Life of Perry.
109, 110. Irving's Life of Goldsmith.
111, 112. Murray's British America.

A NEW Classified and Descriptive Catalogue of HARPER & BROTHERS' Publications has just been issued, comprising a very extensive range of Literature, in its several departments of History, Biography, Philosophy, Travel, Science and Art, the Classics, Fiction, &c.; also, many splendidly Embellished Productions. The selection of works includes not only a large proportion of the most esteemed Literary Productions of our times, but also, in the majority of instances, the best existing authorities on given subjects. This new Catalogue has been constructed with a view to the especial use of persons forming or enriching their Literary Collections, as well as to aid Principals of District Schools and Seminaries of Learning, who may not possess any reliable means of forming a true estimate of any production; to all such it commends itself by its explanatory and critical notices. The valuable collection described in this Catalogue, consisting of about *two thousand volumes*, combines the two-fold advantages of great economy in price with neatness—often elegance of typographical execution, in many instances the rates of publication being scarcely one fifth of those of similar issues in Europe.

*** Copies of this Catalogue may be obtained, free of expense, by application to the Publishers personally, or by letter, post-paid.

To prevent disappointment, it is requested that, whenever books ordered through any bookseller or local agent can not be obtained, applications with remittance be addressed direct to the Publishers, which will be promptly attended to.

YA 03727

14 DAY USE

RETURN TO DESK FROM WHICH BORROWED

LOAN DEPT.

This book is due on the last date stamped below, or
on the date to which renewed.
Renewed books are subject to immediate recall.

■9 Dec '58 B B	
REC'D LD DEC 9 1958	
30 Mar '60 GG	
IN STACKS MAR 16 1960	
REC'D LD JUN 9 1960